CUET

(UG) & Integrated PG
2022

History

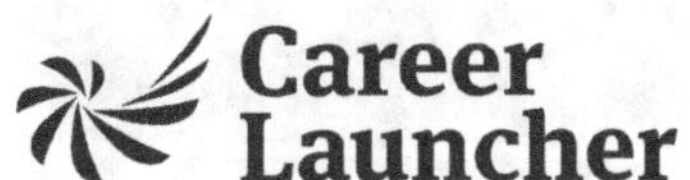

Career
Launcher

Title   : CUET 2022 : History

Language   : English

Editor's Name : Dipak Abhishek

Copyright ©   : 2022 CLIP

No part of this book may be reproduced in a retrieval system or transmitted, in any form or by any means, electronics, mechanical, photocopying, recording, scanning and or without the written permission of the Author/Publisher.

Typeset & Published by :

Career Launcher Infrastructure (P) Ltd.

A-45, Mohan Cooperative Industrial Area, Near Mohan Estate Metro Station, New Delhi - 110044

Marketed by :

G.K. Publications (P) Ltd.

Plot No. 9A, Sector-27A, Mathura Road, Faridabad, Haryana-121003

ISBN   : 978-93-95101-22-6

Printer's Details: Printed in India, New Delhi.

CONTENTS

About CUET

A year ago, it would have been unimaginable that cut-offs in Delhi University would skyrocket to 100% for some of the undergraduate courses! While DU has always been known for its high cut-offs, there are several other universities where the story is no different.

However, the National Education Policy 2020 (NEP) aims to do away with the tyranny of the ever-rising cut-offs by introducing a Common Entrance Test for all the Central Universities in the country. NEP not only proposes a holistic approach in evaluating the students by giving them the option to select subjects based on their interest, but it also aims to simplify the process of admission to higher-education institutes.

To start with, there would be a Common Entrance Test for all the Central Universities, which would be conducted twice a year from 2022. While this might sound like a new concept to many, the fact is, there is already a CUET, which is conducted for the Central Universities established in or after 2009. As many as 14 of them already admit students based on their performance in the entrance test. The CUET scores are also accepted by four state universities of the country.

The proposed CUET aims to assess conceptual understanding and application of knowledge; and also, to lessen the burden of appearing in multiple tests.

CUET Eligibility

Getting into a premier University is every student's dream. The brand value of the University not only facilitates securing a seat in a master's program in a national/international institute, but also helps in getting job offers through campus placements.

Entry to a Central University, in most cases earlier, was based on merit, i.e., marks secured in Class XII Board exams. However, from the academic year 2021, all Central Universities will also consider the CUET score for admissions into their Undergraduate programs.

CUET 2022: Eligibility Criteria

While the official criteria will be learnt once the CUET 2021 notification is released, the stipulations are not expected to change much from those of previous years.

- A candidate must have passed Class XII (10+2) or equivalent from a recognized education Board.
- If the respective Board awards grades (or CGPA), the conversion factor given by the Board must be used to compute the percentage of marks.
- Candidates, who have completed their Class XII in 2021, and have passed the Board exams, will also be eligible to apply for CUET 2022.

Eligibility: Class XII Students

While CUET is for students who have passed the Class XII (or equivalent) Board exams, any student who is appearing for the Class XII Board exam in 2022 is also eligible to apply for CUET 2021. The candidate would be required to produce the marksheets and relevant certificates as mandated by the participating Central University, and follow the timelines provided for admissions.

Key Points

- Each participating Central University is free to decide its own eligibility criteria for admissions.

- The weightages for CUET and Class XII Board exam results(if, applicable) will be at the sole discretion of the Central University, to which admission is being sought.

- As of date, CUET does not have an age limit. However, Central Universities can fix minimum & maximum age limit for admissions to all (or any) of the programs on offer.

Reservation of Seats

As CUET is an entrance exam for admissions to Undergraduate courses at the Central Universities, which have been established under an Act of the Parliament, each Central University must follow the norms set by the Government of India, with respect to intake and reservation of seats.

Generally, the following break-up is followed:

Category	Reservation
Scheduled Castes	15%
Scheduled Tribes	7.5%
Other Backward Classes (Non-Creamy)	27%
Persons with Disability	5%

Some institutions might even have provisions for the Economically Weaker Sections, which can account for 10% of the total seats. These EWS seats are carved out from the Open Category.

To avail of the reservation benefit based on caste (or any other category as specified), a candidate must be able to produce valid documents/certificates to support such claims.

Conclusion

It is essential for every candidate to check the validity of their candidature for CUET, as well as the Central University he/she is applying to. The candidate should be aware of the documents that might be required while applying for the exam, or during the admissions.

CUET 2022 notification is expected in March 2022, and registration is also going to start then.

CUET: Exam Pattern

Examination Structure for CUET (UG) -2022:

CUET (UG) –2022 will consist of the following 4 Sections:

- **Section IA** –13 Languages
- **Section IB** –19 Languages
- **Section II** –27 Domain specific Subjects
- **Section III** –General Test

Choosing options from each Section is not mandatory. Choices should match the requirements of the desired University.

Broad features of CUET (UG) -2022 are as follows:

Section	Subjects/ Tests	Questions to be Attempted	Question Type	Duration
Section IA – Languages	There are 13* different languages. Any of these languages may be chosen.	40 questions to be attempted out of 50 in each language	Language to be tested through Reading Comprehension (based on different types of passages–Factual, Literary and Narrative, [Literary Aptitude and Vocabulary]	45 Minutes for each language
Section IB – Languages	There are 19** Languages. Any other language apart from those offered in Section I A may be chosen.			
Section II - Domain	There are 27*** Domains specific subjects being offered under this Section. A candidate may choose a maximum of Six (06) Domains as desired by the applicable University/Universities.	40 Questions to be attempted out of 50	• Input text can be used for MCQ Based Questions • MCQs based on NCERT Class XII syllabus only	
Section III- General Test	For any such undergraduate programme/ programmes being offered by Universities where a General Test is being used for admission.	60 Questions to be attempted out of 75	• Input text can be used for MCQ Based Questions • General Knowledge, Current Affairs, General Mental Ability, Numerical Ability, Quantitative Reasoning (Simple application of basic mathematical concepts arithmetic/algebra geometry/mensuration/s tat taught till Grade 8), Logical and Analytical Reasoning	

* **Languages (13):** Tamil, Telugu, Kannada, Malayalam, Marathi, Gujarati, Odiya, Bengali, Assamese, Punjabi, English, Hindi and Urdu

** **Languages (19):** *French, Spanish, German, Nepali, Persian, Italian, Arabic, Sindhi, Kashmiri, Konkani, Bodo, Dogri, Maithili, Manipuri, Santhali, Tibetan, Japanese, Russian, Chinese.*

*** **Domain Specific Subjects (27):** 1. Accountancy/ Book Keeping 2. Biology/ Biological Studies/ Biotechnology/Biochemistry 3. Business Studies 4. Chemistry 5. Computer Science/ Informatics Practices 6. Economics/ Business Economics 7. Engineering Graphics 8.Entrepreneurship 9. Geography/Geology 10. History 11. Home Science 12.Knowledge Tradition and Practices of India 13. Legal Studies 14. Environmental Science 15. Mathematics 16. Physical Education/ NCC /Yoga 17.Physics 18.Political Science 19. Psychology 20. Sociology 21. Teaching Aptitude 22. Agriculture 23. Mass Media/ Mass Communication 24. Anthropology 25. Fine Arts/Visual Arts (Sculpture/ Painting)/Commercial Arts, 26. Performing Arts – (i) Dance (Kathak/ Bharatnatyam/Oddisi/ Kathakali/Kuchipudi/ Manipuri (ii) Drama- Theatre (iii) Music General (Hindustani/ Carnatic/ RabindraSangeet/ Percussion/ Non-Percussion), 27. Sanskrit *[For all Shastri (Shastri 3 years/ 4 years Honours) Equivalent to B.A./B.A. Honours courses i.e. Shastri in Veda, Paurohitya (Karmakand), Dharamshastra, Prachin Vyakarana, Navya Vyakarana, Phalit Jyotish, Siddhant Jyotish, Vastushastra, Sahitya,Puranetihas, Prakrit Bhasha,Prachin Nyaya Vaisheshik, Sankhya Yoga, Jain Darshan, Mimansa, AdvaitaVedanta, Vishihstadvaita Vedanta, Sarva Darshan, a candidate may choose Sanskrit as the Domain].*

- A Candidate can choose a maximum of **any 3 languages** from Section IA and Section IB taken together. (One of the languages chosen needs to be in lieu of Domain specific subjects)
- Section II offers 27 Subjects, out of which a candidate may choose a **maximum of 6 Subjects.**
- Section III comprises **General Test.**
- For choosing Languages (upto 3) from Section IA and IB and a maximum of 6 Subjects from Section II and General Test under Section III, the Candidate must refer to the requirements of his/her intended University.

Mode of the Test	Computer Based Test-CBT
Test Pattern	Objective type with Multiple Choice Questions
Medium	13 languages (*Tamil, Telugu, Kannada, Malayalam, Marathi, Gujarati, Odiya, Bengali, Assamese, Punjabi, English, Hindi and Urdu)*
Syllabus	**Section IA & IB:** Language to be tested through Reading Comprehension (based on different types of passages–Factual, Literary and Narrative [Literary Aptitude & Vocabulary]
	Section II : As per NCERT model syllabus as applicable to Class XII only
	Section III : General Knowledge, Current Affairs, General Mental Ability, Numerical Ability, Quantitative Reasoning (Simple application of basic mathematical concepts arithmetic/algebra geometry/mensuration/stat taught till Grade 8), Logical and Analytical Reasoning

Level of questions for CUET (UG) -2022:

All questions in various testing areas will be benchmarked at the level of Class XII only. Students having studied Class XII Board syllabus would be able to do well in CUET (UG) – 2022.

Number of attempts:

If any University permits students of previous years of class XII to take admission in the current year also, such students would also be eligible to appear in CUET (UG) – 2022.

Choice of Languages and Subjects:

Generally the languages/subjects chosen should be the ones that a student has opted in his latest Class XII Board examination. However, if any University permits any flexibility in this regards, the same can be exercised under CUET (UG) -2022 also. Candidates must carefully refer to the eligibility requirements of various Central Universities in this regard. Moreover, if the subject to be studied in the Undergraduate course is not available in the list of **27 Domain Specific Subject** being offered, the Candidate may choose the Subject closest to his choice for e.g. For Biochemistry the candidate may choose Biology.

Candidates are advised to visit the NTA CUET (UG)-2022 official website **https://cuet.samarth.ac.in/** for latest updates regarding the Examination.

CUET Syllabus

CUET Syllabus

Before you start your preparation for any entrance exam, it is important to understand the syllabus. Otherwise, your prep will be directionless, and you might be left wondering where things might have gone wrong!

With more than 1.68 lakh seats on offer for the undergraduate courses at the 54 Central Universities, CUET is one the most competitive examinations. For this very reason, while preparing for the exam, you will need to adopt a structured approach. And in doing that, understanding the syllabus is a critical step.

CUET 2022 Overview

CUET 2022 will be a Computer-Based Test (CBT), commonly referred to as an online exam. However, there is a difference between the two terms: CBT and online. In CBT, the questions are kept constant and simply presented in an online format; whereas in an Online Test, questions are stored as a bank, and the system decides which questions are to be presented to the candidate, based on a pre-defined logic.

CUET 2022 is likely to be a General Ability Test, with focus on English Language, Numerical Ability, Logical & Analytical Reasoning, along with General Awareness and Current Affairs.

CUET 2022 Syllabus

The CUET 2022 exam pattern gives a good idea about what is in store for the candidate and how one needs to prepare for the exam.

- **English Language:** The questions in this section will test one's proficiency in the language, based on comprehension passages, fundamentals of grammar, and vocabulary. In the Comprehension section, candidates will be evaluated on their understanding of a passage and its central theme, meanings of words used therein, etc. The Grammar section entails correcting grammatically incorrect sentences, filling of blanks in sentences with appropriate words, etc. Questions on synonyms & antonyms will check one's command over English vocabulary.
- **Numerical Ability:** Questions on Numerical Ability will test the candidate's knowledge of elementary mathematics. Areas like arithmetic, number system, basics of algebra, and modern maths will be central to these types of questions.
- **Logical & Analytical Reasoning:** This section tests the candidate's ability to identify patterns & logical links, and rectify illogical arguments. It can include a variety of Logical Reasoning questions, such as those on syllogisms, logical sequences, analogies, etc., along with Analytical Reasoning questions on series, directions, clocks & calendars, arrangements, and puzzles to name a few.
- **General Awareness and Current Affairs:** The General Awareness section includes static general knowledge, while questions on Current Affairs will gauge a candidate's knowledge of national & international current affairs.

CUET 2022 may or may not have a section on subject knowledge. Once the exam notification is out in March, there will be more clarity on this matter.

While there is no syllabus explicitly mentioned by CUET, the broad idea is always presented. One must look at the previous years' papers and solve the sample papers available to form a basic understanding.

About University of Delhi

University of Delhi (commonly known as DU) was established in 1922 and is one of the largest Universities in the country. With 16 faculties, 86 academic departments, 90 colleges and 540 programs on offer, Delhi University is no doubt one of the sought-after University in the country.

With 1, 96,000 students enrolled in UG programs, Delhi University is a valued university and constantly ranked among the top in the country. DU bagged 11th Rank in NIRF 2020 and ranked 6th in QS India Rankings 2020. The University has two Campuses: North and South.

DU UG Programs

Delhi University offers several programs at the undergraduate level. With more than 60 constituent colleges, the Delhi University offers many undergraduate courses.

Please refer to the table below for the important undergraduate courses offered by the DU and the intake across each program.

Program	Intake
B. A (Pass)	11249
B. A (Hons) Geography	788
B. A (Hons) Economics	2754
B. A (Hons) History	2791
B. A (Hons) Political Science	3657
B. A (Hons) Sociology	596
B. A (Hons) Psychology	670
B. A (Hons) Applied Psychology	252
B. A (Hons) Social Work	133
B. A (Hons) Philosophy	783
B. A (Hons) English	2886
B. A (Hons) Hindi	2829
B. A (Hons) Sanskrit	1407
B. A (Hons) Punjabi	214
B. A (Hons) Urdu	207
BA(Hons) French	49

Program	Intake
BA(Hons) German	49
BA(Hons) Spanish	49
BA(Hons) Italian	49
B. Com (Hons)	7953
B.Com (Pass)	7854
Program	Intake
B.Sc. (H) Biomedical Science	162
B.Sc. (H) Botany	937
B.Sc. (H) Chemistry	1487
B.Sc. (H) Computer Science	1265
B.Sc. (H) Electronics	624
B.Sc. (H) Mathematics	2428
B.Sc. (H) Physics	1659
B.Sc. (H) Zoology	944
B.Sc. Life Sciences	1515
B.Sc. Physical Science with Chemistry	703
B.Sc. Physical Science with Computer Science	553
B.Sc. Physical Science with Electronics	247
B. Sc (Hons.) Statistics	476
B. Sc. (Prog.) Applied Physical Science Industrial Chemistry	96
B.Sc. (Hons.) Home Science	900
B. Sc. (Hons.) Psychology	57
B.Sc. (H) Food Technology	179
B.Sc. (H)Instrumentation	99
B.Sc. (H) Microbiology	238
B.Sc. (H) Polymer Science	59
B.SC. Mathematical Science	224
B.SC. (Hons.) Biochemistry	146
B.SC. Industrial Chemistry	78
B.Sc. (Prog.) Physical Science	940
B.SC. (Hons.) Geology	98

DU UG Programs Eligibility:

As the University offers multiple programs and separate intake for male and female candidates, it is important to check the university official website regularly to keep oneself updated about the eligibility for each program, which can change.

DU UG Admissions:

Until 2021, Delhi University admitted students on the basis of class XII marks. From the academic year 2022, admissions to UG programs offered Delhi University will be based on CUET. CUET will be a common entrance for admissions to UG programs offered by all the Central Universities in the country.

Delhi University UG Programs Reservation:

DU being a Central University offers reservations in admissions according to central government rules.

Schedule Caste (SC): 15% of the total seats are reserved for students who belong to SC category.

Schedule Tribe (ST): 7.5% of the total seats are reserved for students belonging to ST Category.

Other Backward Classes (OBC): 27% of the total intake is reserved for students from Other Backward Classes (OBC), excluding those from creamy layer.

Economically Weaker Section (EWS): The University has reserved 10% seats for EWS category, in accordance with the directive of Ministry of Education.

Persons with Disability (PWD): 5% of the seats are reserved on horizontal basis for students from PWD category.

About BHU

Banaras Hindu University (BHU), situated in the holy city of Varanasi, was founded by Pandit Madan Mohan Malviya in cooperation with Dr. Annie Besant, in 1916 under the act of Parliament-B.H.U Act, 1915. BHU, which is a Central University, comprises of 6 Institutes, 14 Faculties, 144 academic departments, and 4 Inter-disciplinary centers, spread over 1300 acres. The University consists of 15,000 students, 1700 teachers and 8000 non-teaching staff.

BHU was ranked 3rd among the Universities in India in 2020. According to university submissions for NIRF 2021, BHU has 10, 585 students pursuing UG programs, of which 236 students are foreign nationals.

BHU UG Programs

BHU offers a host of undergraduate programs including medical and engineering. Through its various faculties, BHU offers a range of programs which caters to students learning abilities. The University along with its main campus, also offers the undergraduate courses from the following colleges: Mahila Mahavidyalaya (MMV); Arya Mahila Post Graduate College (AMPGC), Vasant Kanya Mahavidyalaya (VKM); Vasanta College for Women (VCW); DAV Post Graduate College (DAVPGC) and Rajiv Gandhi South Campus (RGSC).

Please refer to the table below for the important undergraduate courses offered by BHU and the intake across each program/campuses.

Faculty of Arts				
Course	Campus	Intake	Status	Duration
B.A (Hons) Arts	Faculty of Arts	765	Co-Ed	3 Years
	Mahila Mahavidyalaya	286	Women	3 Years
	Arya Mahila Post Graduate College	383	Women	3 Years
	Vasant Kanya Mahavidyalaya	286	Women	3 Years
	Vasanta College for Women	412	Women	3 Years
	DAV Post Graduate College	309	Co-Ed	3 Years
Faculty of Social Sciences				
Course	Campus	Intake	Status	Duration
B.A (Hons) Social Sciences [incl. B. A (Hons) Economics]	Faculty of Social Sciences	573	Co-Ed	3 Years
	Mahila Mahavidyalaya	193	Women	3 Years
	Arya Mahila Post Graduate College	383	Women	3 Years
	Vasant Kanya Mahavidyalaya	249	Women	3 Years
	Vasanta College for Women	210	Women	3 Years
	DAV Post Graduate College	326	Co-Ed	3 Years

Faculty of Commerce				
Course	Campus	Intake	Status	Duration
B. Com (Hons)	Faculty of Commerce	286	Co-Ed	3 Years
	Vasant Kanya Mahavidyalaya	96	Women	3 Years
	Arya Mahila Post Graduate College	96	Women	3 Years
	DAV Post Graduate College	227	Co-Ed	3 Years
	Rajiv Gandhi South Campus, Mirzapur	114	Co-Ed	3 Years
B. Com (Hons) Financial Markets Management	Faculty of Commerce	62	Co-Ed	3 Years
	Rajiv Gandhi South Campus, Mirzapur	62	Co-Ed	3 Years

Institute of Science				
Course	Campus	Intake	Status	Duration
B.Sc (Hons) Maths Group	Faculty of Science	573	Co-Ed	3 Years
	Mahila Mahavidyalaya	96	Women	3 Years
B.Sc (Hons) Bio Group	Faculty of Science	383	Co-Ed	3 Years
	Mahila Mahavidyalaya	193	Women	3 Years

Faculty of Visual Arts				
Course	Campus	Intake	Status	Duration
B.F.A (Bachelor of Fine Arts)	Faculty of Visual Arts	96	Co-Ed	4 Years
Faculty of Arts				
Bachelor of Vocation (Retail and Logistics Management)	Rajiv Gandhi South Campus	62	Co-Ed	3 Years
Bachelor of Vocation (Hospitality & Tourism Management)	Rajiv Gandhi South Campus	62	Co-Ed	3 Years
Bachelor of Vocation (Fashion Designing and Event Management)	Rajiv Gandhi South Campus	62	Co-Ed	3 Years
Bachelor of Vocation (Modern Office Management)	Rajiv Gandhi South Campus	62	Co-Ed	3 Years
Bachelor of Vocation (Food Processing & Management)	Rajiv Gandhi South Campus	62	Co-Ed	3 Years
Bachelor of Vocation (Medical Lab. & Technology)	Rajiv Gandhi South Campus	62	Co-Ed	3 Years

BHU UG Programs Eligibility:

Each of the courses have different eligibility for admissions. To be eligible for admissions, one must fulfil all the criteria as laid down by the respective faculties of the University.

B.A (Hons) Arts/ B.A (Hons) Social Sciences: Candidate must not be more than 22 years of age and must have passed class XII or equivalent with minimum 50% marks in aggregate.

B.A (Hons) Economics: Candidate must not be more than 22 years of age and must have passed class XII or equivalent with minimum 50% marks in aggregate along with mathematics as one of the papers.

B. Com (Hons)/B. Com (Hons) Financial Markets Management: Candidate must not be more than 22 years of age and must have passed class XII or equivalent with minimum 50% marks in aggregate with Commerce/ Economics/Maths/Computer Science/Finance/Financial Markets Management as one of the subjects.

B. Sc (Hons) Maths Group: Candidate must not be more than 22 years of age and must have passed class XII or equivalent with minimum 50% marks in aggregate in the subjects Physics, Maths plus any one of the following: Chemistry, Statistics, Geology, Computer Science, Information Technology and Geography and must have passed in each of the concerned three subjects.

B. Sc (Hons) Bio Group: Candidate must not be more than 22 years of age and must have passed class XII or equivalent with minimum 50% marks in aggregate in the subjects Physics, Chemistry plus any one of the following: Biology, Geology and Geography and must have passed in each of the concerned three subjects.

B. F. A (Bachelor of Fine Arts): Candidate must not be more than 22 years of age and must have passed class XII or equivalent with minimum 50% marks in aggregate.

Bachelor of Vocation: Candidate must have passed class XII or equivalent in any stream (Science for Food Processing and Medical Lab Technology) or level 4 NSQF certificate.

BHU UG Admissions:

Until 2021, admissions to BHU UG courses were based on Undergraduate Entrance Test (UET) conducted by the University. From the academic year 2022, admissions to UG programs offered by BHU will be based on CUET, which will replace the UET. CUET will be a common entrance for admissions to UG programs offered by all the Central Universities in the country.

BHU UG Programs Reservation:

BHU being a Central University offers reservations in admissions according to central government rules.

Schedule Caste (SC): 15% of the total seats are reserved for students who belong to SC category.

Schedule Tribe (ST): 7.5% of the total seats are reserved for students belonging to ST Category.

Other Backward Classes (OBC): 27% of the total intake is reserved for students from Other Backward Classes (OBC), excluding those from creamy layer.

Economically Weaker Section (EWS): The University has reserved 10% seats for EWS category, in accordance with the directive of Ministry of Education.

Persons with Disability (PWD): 5% of the seats are reserved on horizontal basis for students from PWD category.

About JNU

Ever wondered which University, the cadets from National Defence Academy (NDA) graduate from? Yes. It is Jawaharlal Nehru University (JNU). JNU started in the year 1969, three years after the act of Parliament in 1966. With several academic centres of JNU declared "Centres of Excellence" by the University Grants Commission, JNU has been ranked No. 1 by National Assessment and Accreditation Council (NAAC). JNU has been ranked No. 2 by National Institutional Ranking Framework (NIRF) 2020 and has been awarded the Best University Award by the President of India in 2017. The European Commission has awarded the Jean Monnet Centre of Excellence for European Union Studies in India (CEEUSI) to Jawaharlal Nehru University in 2018. This is one of the highest international recognition for any European Studies programme.

JNU was the first University to start integrated five-year Master of Arts in Language Courses. JNU actively collaborates with National and International Universities for student and faculty exchange programs.

According to university submissions for NIRF 2020, JNU has 1,048 students pursuing UG programs, of which 46 are foreign nationals.

JNU UG Programs

JNU offers a limited program at the undergraduate level, unlike other universities. The focus at undergraduate has been largely on language courses. In 2018, JNU started two programs in engineering and plans to add a few more specializations in future.

Please refer to the table below for the important undergraduate courses offered by JNU and the intake across each program.

School	Program	Intake	Duration
School of Language, Literature and Cultural Studies	B. A (Hons) Pashto	19	3 Years
	B. A (Hons) Persian	39	3 Years
	B. A (Hons) Arabic	39	3 Years
	B. A (Hons) Japanese	48	3 Years
	B. A (Hons) Korean	39	3 Years
	B. A (Hons) Chinese	44	3 Years
	B. A (Hons) French	48	3 Years
	B. A (Hons) German	48	3 Years
	B. A (Hons) Russian	68	3 Years
	B. A (Hons) Spanish	39	3 Years

School of Sanskrit and Indic Studies	B. Sc - M. Sc Integrated Program in Ayurveda Biology	20	5 Years
School of Engineering	B. Tech in Computer Science and Engineering & MS/M. Tech in Social Sciences/Humanities/Science/Technology	25	5 Years
	B. Tech in Electronics and Communication Engineering & MS/M. Tech in Social Sciences/Humanities/Science/Technology	25	5 Years

JNU UG Programs Eligibility:

Each of the courses have different eligibility for admissions. To be eligible for admissions, one must fulfil all the criteria as laid down by the respective faculties of the University.

B.A (Hons) Language Courses: Candidate must not be less than 17 years of age and must have passed Senior School Certificate (10+2) or equivalent examination with minimum of 45% marks.

B. Sc - M. Sc Integrated Program in Ayurveda Biology: Candidate must not be less than 17 years of age and must have passed Senior School Certificate (10+2) or equivalent examination with minimum of 45% marks.

B. Tech-M. Tech: Based on JEE Mains

JNU UG Admissions:

Until 2021, admissions to JNU UG courses were based on JNU Entrance Examination (JNUEE) conducted by the National Testing Agency (NTA). From the academic year 2022, admissions to UG programs offered by JNU will be based on CUET, which will replace the JNUEE. CUET will be a common entrance for admissions to UG programs offered by all the Central Universities in the country.

JNU UG Programs Reservation:

JNU being a Central University offers reservations in admissions according to central government rules.

Schedule Caste (SC): 15% of the total seats are reserved for students who belong to SC category.

Schedule Tribe (ST): 7.5% of the total seats are reserved for students belonging to ST Category.

Other Backward Classes (OBC): 27% of the total intake is reserved for students from Other Backward Classes (OBC), excluding those from creamy layer. Also, Central List of Caste to be followed.

Economically Weaker Section (EWS): The University has reserved 10% seats for EWS category, in accordance with the directive of Ministry of Education.

Persons with Disability (PWD): 5% of the seats are reserved on horizontal basis for students from PWD category.

About Jamia Milia Islamia

Jamia Milia Islamia (JMI) was founded in 1920 in Aligarh and became a Central University in 1988 by the act of Parliament. Jamia in Urdu stands for University and Milia means National, making Jamia Milia Islamia a National University. Jamia Milia Islamia moved to Delhi in 1925 and shifted to its present campus in Okhla in 1935.

Jamia Milia Islamia is a NAAC accredited University with grade "A" and was placed 10th in NIRF Rankings 2020. According to submissions made by University for NIRF 2021, Jamia Milia Islamia has a total of 5,911 students pursuing undergraduate courses at the University, of which 105 are foreign nationals. The University also manage to place a total of 681 UG students with an average salary ranging 4.2 Lacs-6.0 Lacs.

JMI UG Programs

Jamia Milia Islamia (JMI) offers a host of undergraduate programs for students. Through its various faculties, JMI offers a range of programs which caters to students learning abilities.

Please refer to the table below for the important undergraduate courses offered by Jamia Milia Islamia and the intake across each program.

Faculty	Course	Intake	Duration
Faculty of Humanities and Language	B. A (Hons) English	60	3 Years
	B. A (Hons) Hindi	40	3 Years
	B. A (Hons) Mass Media-Hindi	40	3 Years
	B. A (Hons) History	60	3 Years
	Bachelor of Hotel Management (BHM)	40	3 Years
	Bachelor of Tourism and Travel Management	40	3 Years
	B. Voc (Food Production)	40	3 Years
Faculty of Social Sciences	Bachelor of Arts (B. A)	68	3 Years
	B. Com (Hons)	55	3 Years
	BBA (Bachelor of Business Administration)	44	3 Years
	B. A (Hons) Economics	53	3 Years
	B. A (Hons) Sociology	42	3 Years
	B. A (Hons) Political Science	42	3 Years
	B. A (Hons) Psychology	42	3 Years
Faculty of Natural Sciences	B. Sc (Bachelor of Science)	50	3 Years
	B. Sc Biosciences	40	3 Years
	B. Sc Biotechnology	35	3 Years
	B. Sc (Hons) Chemistry	40	3 Years
	B. A/B. Sc (Hons) Geography	60	3 Years
	B. Sc (Hons) Mathematics	45	3 Years
	B. Sc (Hons) Applied Mathematics	45	3 Years
	B. Sc (Hons) Physics	45	3 Years
Faculty of Fine Arts	Bachelor of Fine Arts (Applied Art)	30	4 Years
	Bachelor of Fine Arts (Art Education)	20	4 Years
	Bachelor of Fine Arts (Painting)	20	4 Years
	Bachelor of Fine Arts (Sculpture)	10	4 Years

JMI UG Programs Eligibility:

Each of the courses have different eligibility for admissions. To be eligible for admissions, one must fulfil all the criteria as laid down by the respective faculties of the University.

B. Com (Hons) /BBA /B. A (Hons) Economics: Candidate must have passed class XII or equivalent with a minimum of 50% marks in five subjects.

BHM/BTTM/B. Voc (Food Production): Candidate must have passed class XII or equivalent with a minimum of 45% marks in five subjects.

B. A (Hons) Mass Media/B. A (Hons) Hindi: Candidate must have passed class XII or equivalent with a minimum of 45% marks in five subjects.

B. Sc/B. Sc (Hons): Candidate must have passed class XII or equivalent with minimum 50% marks in each of the science subjects i.e. Physics, Chemistry and Mathematics and 50% marks in aggregate of best 5-subjects.

JMI UG Admissions:

Until 2021, admissions to JMI UG courses were based on Entrance Test (JMI-ET) conducted by the University. From the academic year 2022, admissions to UG programs offered by JMI will be based on CUET, which will replace the JMI-ET. CUET will be a common entrance for admissions to UG programs offered by all the Central Universities in the country.

JMI UG Programs Reservation:

JMI is a minority reservation-based University and accordingly, seats are reserved for candidates as per the norms laid down by the University.

Muslim Minority: 30% of the total seats are reserved for Muslim applicants; 10% of the total seats are reserved for women applicants who are Muslim; 10% of the total intake is for OBC-NC candidates who are Muslims.

Persons with Disability (PWD): 5% of the seats are reserved for students from PWD category.

Jamia Students: 5% seats in all Undergraduate Programs shall be filled by internal students of Jamia who have passed their qualifying examination of the concerned programme (X or XII) from Jamia Schools as regular students.

In addition, Jamia Milia Islamia has supernumerary seats for Kashmiri Migrants and students from Jammu and Kashmir.

About Aligarh Muslim University

Aligarh Muslim University also referred as AMU was established by Sir Syed Ahmad Khan in 1875. The University started as Muhammadan Anglo-Oriental College and became a University (AMU) in 1920. The university has been ranked 801–1000 in the QS World University Rankings of 2021 and 17 in India by the National Institutional Ranking Framework in 2020.

Aligarh Muslim University is institution of national importance, under the seventh schedule of the Constitution of India.

AMU UG Programs

Aligarh Muslim University offers several programs at the undergraduate level. With 7 constituent colleges, the Aligarh Muslim University offers many undergraduate courses.

Please refer to the table below for the important undergraduate courses offered by the AMU and the intake across each program.

Course	Intake	Duration
B. Sc (Hons) Home Science	30*	3 Years
B.Sc (Hons) Agriculture	40	4 Years
B. A (Hons) Arabic	20+10*	3 Years
B. A (Hons) Communicative English	15+20*	3 Years
B. A (Hons) English	40+35*	3 Years
B. A (Hons) Hindi	40+25*	3 Years
B. A (Hons) Geography	50+20*	3 Years
B. A (Hons) Linguistics	20+25*	3 Years
B. A (Hons) Persian	15+25*	3 Years
B. A (Hons) Philosophy	20+10*	3 Years
B. A (Hons) Quaranic Studies	10+10*	3 Years
B. A (Hons) Sanskrit	15+10*	3 Years
B. A (Hons) Urdu	40+50*	3 Years
Bachelor of Fine Arts	15+15*	3 Years
B. Com (Hons)	180+100*	3 Years
B. Voc Production Technology	50	3 Years
B Voc Polymer and Coating Technology	50	3 Years
B. Voc Fashion Design and Garment Technology	50	3 Years
B. A (Hons) Chinese	20	3 Years
B. A (Hons) French	20	3 Years
B. A (Hons) German	20	3 Years

B. A (Hons) Russian	20	3 Years
B. A (Hons) Spanish	20	3 Years
B. Sc (Hons) Biochemistry	30+30*	3 Years
B. Sc (Hons) Botany	60+40*	3 Years
B. Sc (Hons) Zoology	60+45*	3 Years
B. Sc (Hons) Physics	120+35*	3 Years
B. Sc (Hons) Chemistry	120+65*	3 Years
B. Sc (Hons) Mathematics	120+40*	3 Years
B. Sc (Hons) Geography	45+30*	3 Years
B. Sc (Hons) Geology	100+30*	3 Years
B. Sc (Hons) Statistics	60+30*	3 Years
B. Sc (Hons) Industrial Chemistry	20+10*	3 Years
B. Sc (Hons) Computer Applications	40+20*	3 Years

AMU UG Programs Eligibility:

As the University offers multiple programs and separate intake for male and female candidates, it is important to check the university official website regularly to keep oneself updated about the eligibility for each program, which can change.

AMU UG Admissions:

Until 2021, AMU conducted its own entrance test to admit students for the UG programs. From the academic year 2022, admissions to UG programs offered by Aligarh Muslim University will be based on CUET. CUET will be a common entrance for admissions to UG programs offered by all the Central Universities in the country.

University of Allahabad UG Programs Reservation:

Allahabad University being a Central University offers reservations in admissions according to central government rules. Kindly check the university website for further details.

HISTORY

CHAPTER 1

THEME ONE

Bricks, Beads and Bones

The Harappan Civilisation

What we know about the Harappan civilisation (archaeological evidence)

- The Harappan seal Made of a stone is called steatite

- The Indus valley civilisation is also called the Harappan culture.

- Objects that are found include seals, beads, weights, stone blades and baked bricks.

- These objects were found from areas as far apart as Afghanistan, Jammu, Baluchistan (Pakistan) and Gujarat.

- Harappa, the first site where this unique culture was discovered is dated between c. 2600 and 1900 BCE.

- There were earlier and later cultures, often called Early Harappan and Late Harappan, in the same area.

- Early Harappa culture – Before 2600 BCE

- Mature Harappa culture – 2600 BCE to 1900 BCE and

- Late Harappa culture – After 1900 BCE

- The Harappan civilisation is sometimes called the Mature Harappan culture to distinguish it from these cultures.

Harappan culture (beginning)

- Prior to the Mature Harappan culture, there were several archaeological cultures associated with distinctive pottery, agriculture, pastoralism, and crafts.

- Settlements were generally small

- There were virtually no large buildings.

- There was a break between the Early Harappan and the Harappan civilisation

- The break is evident from large-scale burning at some sites, as well as the abandonment of certain settlements.

- Mature Harappan culture developed in some of the areas occupied by the Early Harappan cultures.

- The Harappans ate a wide range of plant and animal products, including fish.

- Grains found at Harappan sites include wheat, barley, lentil, chickpea and sesame.

- Millets are found from sites in Gujarat. Traces of rice are relatively rare.

- Animal bones found at Harappan sites include those of cattle, sheep, goat, buffalo and pig.

- Animals were domesticated.

- Bones of wild species such as boar, deer and gharial are also found.

- Bones of fish and fowl are also found.

Agricultural technologies

- Prevalence of agriculture is indicated by finds of grain.

- Representations on seals and terracotta sculpture indicate that the bull was known

- Oxen were used for ploughing.

- Terracotta models of the plough have been found at sites in Cholistan and at Banawali (Haryana).

- Evidence of a ploughed field at Kalibangan (Rajasthan), associated with Early Harappan levels

- Two different crops were grown together.

- Most Harappan sites are located in semi-arid lands, where irrigation was probably required for agriculture.

- Traces of canals have been found at the Harappan site of Shortughai in Afghanistan, but not in Punjab or Sind.

- It is also likely that water drawn from wells was used for irrigation.

- Water reservoirs found in Dholavira (Gujarat) may have been used to store water for agriculture.

The plight of Harappa

- Harappa was the first site to be discovered but it was badly destroyed by brick robbers.
- Thus, many of the ancient structures at the site were damaged. In contrast, Mohenjodaro was far better preserved.

Mohenjodaro: A Planned Urban Centre

- The most unique feature of the Harappan civilisation was the development of urban centres.
- Mohenjodaro is the most well-known site (the first site to be discovered was Harappa)
- The settlement is divided into two sections, one smaller but higher(Citadel)and the other much larger but lower(Lower Town)

Citadel

- The Citadel owes its height to the fact that buildings were constructed on mud brick platforms.
- It was walled, which meant that it was physically separated from the Lower Town.

Citadels (Variations)

- While most Harappan settlements have a small high western part and a larger lower eastern section, there are variations.
- At sites such as Dholavira and Lothal (Gujarat), the entire settlement was fortified, and sections within the town were also separated by walls.
- The Citadel within Lothal was not walled off, but was built at a height.

Citadel (used for special public purposes)

- Excavated at Mohenjo-daro in Sindh, Pakistan.
- This Citadel include the warehouse and the Great Bath.
- The Great Bath was a large rectangular tank in a courtyard surrounded by a corridor on all four sides.
- The Great Bath is located at the centre of the Citadel, is made of fine baked waterproof mud bricks and a thick layer of bitumen (natural tar – presumably to keep water from seeping through the walls), which indicates that it was used for holding water.
- This huge deep bath could have been a place for ritual bathing or religious ceremonies.
- It is the earliest public water tank of the ancient world.
- Adjacent to it are a well that was used to supply water to the bath.

Lower Town

- The Lower Town was also walled.
- Several buildings were built on platforms, which served as foundations.

- The settlement was first planned and then implemented accordingly.
- Other signs of planning include bricks, which, whether sun-dried or baked, were of a standardised ratio, where the length and breadth were four times and twice the height respectively.
- Such bricks were used at all Harappan settlements.

Laying out drains

- One of the most distinctive features of Harappan cities was the carefully planned drainage system.
- In Lower Town roads and streets were laid out along an approximate "grid" pattern, intersecting at right angles.
- Streets with drains were laid out first and then houses built along them.
- Every house was connected to the street drains.
- Drainage systems were not unique to the larger cities, but were found in smaller settlements as well.
- At Lothal for example, while houses were built of mud bricks, drains were made of burnt bricks.

Domestic architecture

- The Lower Town at Mohenjodaro provides examples of residential buildings.
- Many were centred on a courtyard, with rooms on all sides.
- The courtyard was probably the centre of activities such as cooking and weaving, particularly during hot and dry weather.
- No windows in the walls along the ground level.
- The main entrance does not give a direct view of the interior or the courtyard (taking care of the concern of privacy)
- Every house had its own bathroom paved with bricks, with drains connected through the wall to the street drains.
- Some houses have remains of staircases to reach a second storey or the roof.
- Many houses had wells, often in a room that could be reached from the outside and perhaps used by passers-by.

Burials

- At burials in Harappan sites the dead were generally laid in pits.
- Some graves contain pottery and ornaments
- Jewellery has been found in burials of both men and women.

- In the excavations at the cemetery in Harappa in the mid-1980s, an ornament consisting of three shell rings, a jasper (a kind of semi-precious stone) bead and hundreds of micro beads was found near the skull of a male.
- In some instances the dead were buried with copper mirrors.
- Harappans did not believe in burying precious things with the dead.

Artefacts

- Rare objects made of valuable materials are generally concentrated in large settlements like Mohenjodaro and Harappa and are rarely found in the smaller settlements.
- For example, miniature pots of faience, perhaps used as perfume bottles, are found mostly in Mohenjodaro and Harappa, and there are none from small settlements like Kalibangan.(*Faience -a material made of ground sand or silica mixed with colour and a gum and then fired*)
- Gold too was rare, and as at present, probably precious – all the gold jewellery found at Harappan sites was recovered from hoards (*Hoards are objects kept carefully by people, often inside containers such as pots*)

Craft Production

- Chanhudaro is a tiny devoted to craft production, including bead-making, shell-cutting, metal-working, seal-making and weight-making.
- The variety of materials used to make beads is remarkable: stones like carnelian (of a beautiful red colour), jasper, crystal, quartz and steatite; metals like copper, bronze and gold; and shell, faience and terracotta or burnt clay.
- Some beads were made of two or more stones, cemented together, some of stone with gold caps.
- Specialised drills have been found at Chanhudaro, Lothal and more recently at Dholavira.
- Finished products (such as beads) from Chanhudaro and Lothal were taken to the large urban centres such as Mohenjodaro and Harappa
- Nageshwar and Balakot settlements are near the coast – These were specialised centres for making shell objects – including bangles, ladles and inlay, which were taken to other settlements.
- Craft production was undertaken in large cities such as Mohenjodaro and Harappa.

Procurement of Materials used for craft production

- Clay were locally available
- stone, timber and metal had to be procured from outside the alluvial plain.

- Terracotta toy models of bullock carts suggest that this was one important means of transporting goods and people across land routes.
- Riverine routes along the Indus and its tributaries, as well as coastal routes were also probably used.
- Shortughai (Afghanista) - source of lapis lazuli, a blue stone that was apparently very highly valued
- Lothal which was near sources of carnelian (from Bharuch in Gujarat), steatite (from south Rajasthan and north Gujarat) and metal (from Rajasthan).
- Khetri region of Rajasthan (for copper) and south India (for gold).
- Copper was also probably brought from Oman
- Mesopotamian texts datable to the third millennium BCE refer to copper coming from a region called Magan, perhaps a name for Oman
- Mesopotamian texts mention contact with regions named Dilmun (probably the island of Bahrain), Magan and Meluhha, possibly the Harappan region.

Seals, Script, Weights

Seals and sealings

- Seals and sealings were used to facilitate long-distance communication.
- Harappan seals usually have a line of writing, probably containing the name and title of the owner.
- The script remains undeciphered to date
- It is apparent that the script was written from right to left

Weights

- Exchanges were regulated by a precise system of weights, usually made of a stone called chert and generally cubical with no markings.
- The lower denominations of weights were binary (1, 2, 4, 8, 16, 32, etc. up to 12,800), while the higher denominations followed the decimal system.
- The smaller weights were probably used for weighing jewellery and beads.
- Metal scale-pans have also been found.

Ancient Authority

- If we look for a centre of power or for depictions of people in power, archaeological records provide no immediate answers.

Theories assumed by archaeologists

1. Harappan society had no rulers, and that everybody enjoyed equal status.
2. There was no single ruler but several, that Mohenjodaro had a separate ruler, Harappa another, and so forth.
3. There was a single state, given the similarity in

artefacts, the evidence for planned settlements, the standardised ratio of brick size, and the establishment of settlements near sources of raw material (the third theory seems the most plausible)

The End of the Civilisation

- There is evidence that by c. 1800 BCE most of the Mature Harappan sites in regions such as Cholistan had been abandoned.

- Several explanations have been put forward. These range from climatic change, deforestation, excessive floods, the shifting and/or drying up of rivers, to overuse of the landscape.

- Some of these "causes" may hold for certain settlements, but they do not explain the collapse of the entire civilisation.

Discovering the Harappan Civilisation

- Cunningham, the first Director-General of the ASI, began archaeological excavations in the mid-nineteenth century

- Seals were discovered at Harappa by archaeologists such as Daya Ram Sahni in the early decades of the twentieth century

- Another archaeologist, Rakhal Das Banerji found similar seals at Mohenjodaro

- In 1924, John Marshall, Director-General of the ASI, announced the discovery of a new civilisation in the Indus valley to the world.

Techniques used for excavation

- Generally, the lowest layers are the oldest and the highest are the most recent. The study of these layers is called stratigraphy.

- Artefacts found in layers can be assigned to specific cultural periods and can thus provide the cultural sequence for a site.

- An extensive survey in Kutch has revealed a number of Harappan settlements and explorations in Punjab and Haryana have added to the list of Harappan sites.

- While Kalibangan, Lothal, Rakhi Garhi and most recently Dholavira have been discovered, explored and excavated as part of these efforts, fresh explorations continue.

Exercise

Level - 1

1. Which of the following settlements was exclusively devoted to craft productions?
   - (a) Chanhudaro
   - (b) Mohenjodaro
   - (c) Lothal
   - (d) Dholavira

2. The first site to be discovered was
   - (a) Mohenjodaro
   - (b) Harappa
   - (c) Lothal
   - (d) Kalibangan

3. The Harappan seal was made up of which of the following materials?
   - (a) Copper
   - (b) Steatite
   - (c) Bronze
   - (d) None of the above

4. Mesopotamian texts mention trade and commerce with which of the following regions?
   - (a) Dilmun
   - (b) Magan
   - (c) Meluhha
   - (d) All of the above

5. Which of the following Animal bones was not found at Harappan sites?
   - (a) Cattle
   - (b) Sheep
   - (c) Buffalo
   - (d) Cow

6. Which of the following Grains was found at Harappan sites ?
   - (a) Wheat
   - (b) Barley
   - (c) Lentil
   - (d) All of the above

7. Millets are found from sites of which of the following regions?
   - (a) Gujrat
   - (b) Sindh
   - (c) Punjab
   - (d) Rajasthan

8. Select the wrong statements with respect to Harappa civilization
   - (a) There were no evidence of rice cultivation
   - (b) Animals were domesticated.
   - (c) Bones of wild species such as boar, deer are found.
   - (d) Bones of fish and fowl are also found.

9. Chanhudaro and Lothal were famous for which of the following craft productions?
   - (a) Beads
   - (b) Pottery
   - (c) Terracotta toy
   - (d) Stone artefacts

10. Archaeologists have also found evidence of a ploughed field at Kalibangan (Rajasthan), associated with which of the following cultures ?
    - (a) Early Harappa culture
    - (b) Mature Harappa culture
    - (c) Late Harappa culture
    - (d) None of the above

11. Most of the Harappan sites were located in
    - (a) Semi-arid regions
    - (b) Arid regions
    - (c) Alluvial planes
    - (d) Doab belt

12. Traces of canals have been found at which of the following Harappan sites?
    - (a) Shortughai (Afghanistan)
    - (b) Punjab or Sind
    - (c) Banawali (Haryana)
    - (d) Kalibangan (Rajasthan)

13. Water reservoirs found in which of the following Harappan sites?
    - (a) Baluchistan (Pakistan)
    - (b) Dholavira (Gujarat)
    - (c) Mohenjodaro
    - (d) Banawali (Haryana).

Level - 2

14. There was a break between which of the following civilisations?
    - (a) The Early Harappan and the Harappan civilisation
    - (b) The Harappan and the Mature Harappan civilisation
    - (c) The Mature Harappan and the Late Harappan cultures
    - (d) All of the above

15. Mesopotamian texts refer to copper coming from a region called Magan.

    Megan represents which of the following regions?
    - (a) Egypt
    - (b) Oman
    - (c) Bahrain
    - (d) Harappan region

16. Which of the following is the most plausible theories assumed by archaeologists?
    - (a) Harappan society had no rulers, and that everybody enjoyed equal status.
    - (b) There was no single ruler but several
    - (c) There was a single state
    - (d) None of the above

17. Which of the following statements is true about Citadels?

(a) The settlements were smaller but higher than Lower Town

(b) Citadels were not physically separated from the Lower Town.

(c) The buildings in citadels were constructed on wooden platforms

(d) All statements are true

18. The roads and streets of which of the following settlements were laid out along an approximate "grid" pattern, intersecting at right angles.

(a) Lower Town

(b) Citadel

(c) great bath area of Mohenjodaro

(d) Both (a) and (b)

19. Which of the following Harappan settlements were fortified entirely?

(a) Dholavira   (b) Lothal

(c) Kalibangan   (d) Both (a) and (b)

20. Which of the following settlement is located near the coast.

(a) Chanhudaro

(b) Dholavira

(c) Nageshwar

(d) Mohenjodaro

21. Which of the following was an important means of transporting goods and people across land routes in Harappan civilization?

(a) Horses   (b) Bullock carts

(c) Unicorns   (d) None of the above

22. The Harappans procured lapis lazuli, a blue stone that was apparently very highly valued materials, for craft production from which of the following regions?

(a) Afghanistan   (b) South India region

(c) Mesopotamia   (d) Egypt

23. Find the incorrect statement about the system of weights in Harappan civilization

(a) The lower denominations of weights were binary

(b) The higher denominations followed the decimal system.

(c) The weights were made of a stone called chert

(d) The weights were rectangular in shape with no markings.

24. Find the correct statement about The Great Bath

(a) The Great Bath was a large circular tank in a courtyard

(b) It was located at the centre of the Lower town

(c) It was meant for some kind of a special ritual bath.

(d) It is made of fine baked waterproof thick layer of bitumen without the use of any single mud bricks

Answers

Level-1

| 1. (a) | 2. (b) | 3. (b) | 4. (d) | 5. (d) | 6. (d) | 7. (a) | 8. (a) | 9. (a) | 10. (a) |

| 11. (a) | 12. (a) | 13. (b) |

Level-2

| 14. (a) | 15. (b) | 16. (c) | 17. (a) | 18. (a) | 19. (d) | 20. (c) | 21. (b) | 22. (a) | 23. (d) |

| 24. (c) |

Explanations

Level - 1

1. a • Chanhudaro is a tiny settlement almost exclusively devoted to craft production, including bead-making, shell-cutting, metal-working, seal-making and weight-making.

2. b • 1921 M.S. Vats begins excavations at Harappa

  1925 Excavations begin at Mohenjodaro

• Mohenjodaro is the most well-known site, the first site to be discovered was Harappa.

3. b • The Harappan seal is possibly the most distinctive artefact of the Harappan or Indus valley civilisation. Made of a stone called steatite

4. d • Mesopotamian texts mention contact with regions named Dilmun (probably the island of Bahrain), Magan and Meluhha, possibly the Harappan region.

5. d • Animal bones found at Harappan sites include those of cattle, sheep, goat, buffalo and pig.

6. d • Grains found at Harappan sites include wheat, barley, lentil, chickpea and sesame.

7. a • Millets are found from sites in Gujarat.

8. a • Animals were domesticated.

• Bones of wild species such as boar, deer and *gharial* are also found

• Bones of fish and fowl are also found.

• Finds of rice are relatively rare.

9. a • Chanhudaro and Lothal were devoted to craft production, including bead-making, shell-cutting, metal-working, seal-making and weight-making.

10. a • Archaeologists have also found evidence of a ploughed field at Kalibangan (Rajasthan), associated with Early Harappan levels

11. a • Most Harappan sites are located in semi-arid lands, where irrigation was probably required for agriculture.

12. a • Traces of canals have been found at the Harappan site of Shortughai in Afghanistan, but not in Punjab or Sind.

13. b • Water reservoirs found in Dholavira (Gujarat) may have been used to store water for agriculture.

Level - 2

14. a • There were earlier and later cultures, often called Early Harappan and Late Harappan, in the same area.

• The Harappan civilisation is sometimes called the Mature Harappan culture to distinguish it from these cultures.

• It appears that there was a break between the Early Harappan and the Harappan civilisation, evident from large-scale burning at some sites, as well as the abandonment of certain settlements.

15. b • Mesopotamian texts datable to the third millennium BCE refer to copper coming from a region called Magan, perhaps a name for Oman

16. c • The most plausible theory -There was a single state, given the similarity in artefacts, the evidence for planned settlements, the standardised ratio of brick size, and the establishment of settlements near sources of raw material

17. a • The settlement is divided into two sections, one smaller but higher and the other much larger but lower.

• Archaeologists designate these as the Citadel and the Lower Town respectively.

• The Citadel owes its height to the fact that buildings were constructed on mud brick platforms.

• It was walled, which meant that it was physically separated from the Lower Town.

18. a • One of the most distinctive features of Harappan cities was the carefully planned drainage system.

• In the Lower Town, the roads and streets were laid out along an approximate "grid" pattern, intersecting at right angles. It seems that streets with drains were laid out first and then houses built along them.

19. d • While most Harappan settlements have a small high western part and a larger lower eastern section, there are variations. At sites such as Dholavira and Lothal (Gujarat), the entire settlement was fortified, and sections within the town were also separated by walls.

20. c • Nageshwar and Balakot settlements are near the coast.

• These were specialised centres for making shell objects

21. b • Terracotta toy models of bullock carts suggest that this was one important means of transporting goods and people across land routes.

22. a • The Harappans procured materials for craft production in various ways.

• For instance, they established settlements such as Shortughai, in far-off Afghanistan, near the best source of lapis lazuli, a blue stone that was apparently very highly valued

23. d • Exchanges were regulated by a precise system of weights usually made of a stone called chert and generally cubical with no markings.

• Lower denominations of weights were binary (1, 2, 4, 8, 16, 32, etc. up to 12,800), while the higher denominations followed the decimal system.

24. c • Excavated at Mohenjo-daro in Sindh, Pakistan.

• This Citadel include the warehouse and the Great Bath.

• The Great Bath was a large rectangular tank in a courtyard surrounded by a corridor on all four sides.

• The Great Bath is located at the centre of the Citadel, is made of fine baked waterproof mud bricks and a thick layer of bitumen.

CHAPTER 2

THEME TWO
Kings, Farmers and Towns
Early States and Economies (c. 600 BCE-600 CE)

Developments after the end of the Harappan civilisation.

- Rigveda was composed by people living along the Indus and its tributaries.
- Agricultural settlements emerged in north India, the Deccan Plateau, and parts of Karnataka.
- Evidence of pastoral populations in the Deccan and further south.
- New modes of disposal of the dead, including the making of elaborate stone structures known as megaliths
- In many cases, the dead were buried with a rich range of iron tools and weapons.

Developments in Indian epigraphy (1830s.)

- James Prinsep, an officer in the mint of the East India Company, deciphered Brahmi and Kharosthi, two scripts used in the earliest inscriptions and coins.
- Most of these mentioned a king referred to as Piyadassi – meaning "pleasant to behold"
- There were a few inscriptions which also referred to the king as Asoka, one of the most famous rulers known from Buddhist texts.

Inscriptions

- Inscriptions are writings engraved on hard surfaces such as stone, metal or pottery.
- They usually record the achievements, activities or ideas of those who commissioned them
- It includes the exploits of kings, or donations made by women and men to religious institutions.
- Inscriptions are virtually permanent records, some of which carry dates.
- Others are dated on the basis of palaeography or styles of writing, with a fair amount of precision.
- The earliest inscriptions were in Prakrit, a name for languages used by ordinary people.

- Ajatasattu and Asoka, known from Prakrit texts and inscriptions
- Pali, Tamil and Sanskrit, were also used to write inscriptions and texts.

The Earliest States : The sixteen mahajanapadas

- The sixth century BCE is an era associated with early states, cities, the growing use of iron, the development of coinage, etc.
- It also witnessed the growth of diverse systems of thought, including Buddhism and Jainism.
- Early Buddhist and Jaina texts mention, amongst other things, sixteen states known as mahajanapadas.
- Most mahajanapadas were ruled by kings, some, known as ganas or sanghas, were oligarchies,where power was shared by a number of men, often collectively called rajas. Both Mahavira and the Buddha belonged to such ganas.
- In the case of the Vajji sangha, the rajas probably controlled resources such as land collectively.
- Each mahajanapada had a capital city, which was often fortified.
- Janapada means the land where a jana (a people, clan or tribe) sets its foot or settles. It is a word used in both Prakrit and Sanskrit.
- From c. sixth century BCE onwards, Brahmanas began composing Sanskrit texts known as the Dharmasutras.
- These laid down norms for rulers (as well as for other social categories), who were ideally expected to be Kshatriyas
- Rulers were advised to collect taxes and tribute from cultivators, traders and artisans.
- Raids on neighbouring states were recognised as a legitimate means of acquiring wealth.

First amongst the sixteen: Magadha

- Between the sixth and the fourth centuries BCE, Magadha (in present-day Bihar) became the most powerful mahajanapada.
- Magadha was a region where agriculture was especially productive.
- Elephants, an important component of the army, were found in forests in the region.
- Also, the Ganga and its tributaries provided a means of cheap and convenient communication.
- Early Buddhist and Jaina writers who wrote about Magadha attributed its power to the policies of individuals: ruthlessly ambitious kings of whom Bimbisara, Ajatasattu and Mahapadma Nanda are the best known
- Initially, Rajagaha (the Prakrit name for present- day Rajgir in Bihar) was the capital of Magadha.
- Rajagaha was a fortified settlement, located amongst hills.
- Later, in the fourth century BCE, the capital was shifted to Pataliputra, present-day Patna

Languages and scripts

- Most Asokan inscriptions were in the Prakrit language while those in the northwest of the subcontinet were in Aramaic and Greek.
- Most Prakrit inscriptions were written in the Brahmi script; however, some, in the northwest, were written in Kharosthi.
- The Aramaic and Greek scripts were used for inscriptions in Afghanistan.

An Early Empire

- The growth of Magadha culminated in the emergence of the Mauryan Empire.
- Chandragupta Maurya, who founded the empire (c. 321 BCE), extended control as far northwest as Afghanistan and Baluchistan, and his grandson Asoka, conquered Kalinga (present-day coastal Orissa).

Sources to reconstruct the history of the Mauryan Empire.

- Megasthenes (a Greek ambassador to the court of Chandragupta Maurya)
- Arthashastra (composed by Kautilya or Chanakya, traditionally believed to be the minister of Chandragupta.)
- The Mauryas are mentioned in later Buddhist, Jaina and Puranic literature, as well as in Sanskrit literary works.
- The inscriptions of Asoka (c. 272/268-231 BCE) on rocks and pillars
- Asoka was the first ruler who inscribed his messages to his subjects and officials on stone surfaces – natural rocks as well as polished pillars.
- He used the inscriptions to proclaim what he understood to be dhamma.
- This included respect towards elders, generosity towards Brahmanas

Administrative system

- There were five major political centres in the empire – the capital Pataliputra and the provincial centres of Taxila, Ujjayini, Tosali and Suvarnagiri, all mentioned in Asokan inscriptions.
- It is likely that administrative control was strongest in areas around the capital and the provincial centres.
- These centres were carefully chosen, both Taxila and Ujjayini being situated on important long-distance trade routes, while Suvarnagiri (literally, the golden mountain) was possibly important for tapping the gold mines of Karnataka.
- Megasthenes mentions a committee with six subcommittees for coordinating military activity.
- Of these, one looked after the navy, the second managed transport and provisions, the third was responsible for foot-soldiers, the fourth for horses, the fifth for chariots and the sixth for elephants.
- Asoka also tried to hold his empire together by propagating dhamma
- Special officers, known as the dhamma mahamatta, were appointed to spread the message of dhamma.
- The Mauryan Empire lasted for about 150 years, which is not a very long time in the vast span of the history of the subcontinent.

New Notions of Kingship

- By the second century BCE, new kingdoms emerged in the Deccan and further south, including the chiefdoms of the Cholas, Cheras and Pandyas in Tamilakam (the name of the ancient Tamil country, which included parts of present-day Andhra Pradesh and Kerala, in addition to Tamil Nadu)
- We know about these states from a variety of sources (eg -early Tamil Sangam texts)

Chiefs and chiefdoms

- A chief is a powerful man whose position may or may not be hereditary.
- He derives support from his kinfolk.
- His functions may include performing special rituals, leadership in warfare, and arbitrating disputes.
- He receives gifts from his subordinates (unlike kings who usually collect taxes) and often distributes these amongst his supporters.
- Generally, there are no regular armies and officials in chiefdoms.

Divine King

- One means of claiming high status was to identify with a variety of deities. This strategy is best exemplified by the
- Kushanas (c. first century BCE- first century CE), who ruled over a vast kingdom extending from Central Asia to northwest India.
- The notions of kingship they wished to project are perhaps best evidenced in their coins and sculpture.
- Colossal statues of Kushana rulers have been found installed in a shrine at Mat near Mathura (Uttar Pradesh).
- Similar statues have been found in a shrine in Afghanistan as well.
- The Kushanas considered themselves godlike.
- Many Kushana rulers also adopted the title devaputra, or "son of god"

Gupta Empire.

- By the fourth century there is evidence of larger states, including the Gupta Empire.
- Many of these depended on samantas, men who maintained themselves through local resources including control over land.
- They offered homage and provided military support to rulers.
- Powerful samantas could become kings: conversely, weak rulers might find themselves being reduced to positions of subordination.
- Source - literature, coins and inscriptions, including prashastis, composed in praise of kings in particular, and patrons in general, by poets.
- The Prayaga Prashasti (also known as the Allahabad Pillar Inscription) composed in Sanskrit by Harishena, the court poet of Samudragupta, arguably the most powerful of the Gupta rulers (c. fourth century CE)

A Changing Countryside

- Source of information - Jatakas (written in Pali around the middle of the first millennium CE) and the Panchatantra.

Relationship between a king and his subjects (villagers)

- Kings frequently tried to fill their coffers by demanding high taxes
- To escape from this situation, people abandoned their village and went to live in the forest. (as mentioned in Jataka story)
- Strategies aimed at increasing production to meet growing demand for taxes adopted
- Transplantation is used for paddy cultivation in areas where water is plentiful.

Uneven benefits of increased production

- There was a growing differentiation amongst people engaged in agriculture – stories, especially within the Buddhist tradition, refer to landless agricultural labourers, small peasants, as well as large landholders.
- The term *gahapati* was often used in Pali texts to designate the second and third categories.
- The large landholders, as well as the village headman (whose position was often hereditary), emerged as powerful figures, and often exercised control over other cultivators.
- Early Tamil literature (the Sangam texts) also mentions different categories of people living in the villages – large landowners or *vellalar*, ploughmen or *uzhavar* and slaves or *adimai*.

Sudarshana lake (Gujarat)

- The Sudarshana lake was an artificial reservoir.
- Souce of information - rock inscription (c. second century CE) in Sanskrit, composed to record the achievements of the Shaka ruler Rudradaman.
- The inscription mentions that the lake, with embankments and water channels, was built by a local governor during the rule of the Mauryas.
- Rudradaman, repaired the lake using his own resources, without imposing any tax on his subjects.
- Another inscription on the same rock (c. fifth century) mentions how one of the rulers of the Gupta dynasty got the lake repaired once again.

Terminologies

Gahapati

- A gahapati was the owner, master or head of a household, who exercised control over the women, children, slaves and workers who shared a common residence.
- He was also the owner of the resources – land, animals and other things – that belonged to the household.

Manusmrti

- It is one of the best-known legal texts of early India, written in Sanskrit and compiled between c. second century BCE and c. second century CE.

Agrahara

- An *agrahara* was land granted to a Brahmana, who was usually exempted from paying land revenue and other dues to the king, and was often given the right to collect these dues from the local people.

Land grants and new rural elites

- Grants of land being made, many of which were recorded in inscriptions. (stone or copper plates)
- It given as a record of the transaction to those who received the land.

- The records that have survived are generally about grants to religious institutions or to Brahmanas.
- Most inscriptions were in Sanskrit.
- The inscription also gives us an idea about rural populations – these included Brahmanas and peasants

Towns and Trade

Emergence of new Urban centres (sixth century BCE) -All major towns were located along routes of communication.

- Pataliputra - riverine routes.
- Ujjayini - land routes
- Puhar - near the coast
- Mathura were bustling centres of commercial, cultural and political activity.

Artefacts recovered

- Fine pottery bowls and dishes, with a glossy finish, known as Northern Black Polished Ware and ornaments, tools, weapons, vessels, figurines, made of a wide range of materials – gold, silver, copper, bronze, ivory, glass, shell and terracotta.

Pataliputra

- It began as a village known as Pataligrama.
- In the fifth century BCE, the Magadhan rulers decided to shift their capital from Rajagaha to this settlement and renamed it.
- By the fourth century BCE, it was the capital of the Mauryan Empire and one of the largest cities in Asia.
- Subsequently, its importance apparently declined.
- When the Chinese pilgrim Xuan Zang visited the city in the seventh century CE, he found it in ruins, and with a very small population.

Trade in the subcontinent and beyond

- From the sixth century BCE, land and river routes criss-crossed the subcontinent and extended in various directions
- Rulers often attempted to control these routes, possibly by offering protection for a price.
- Those who traversed these routes included peddlers who probably travelled on foot and merchants who travelled with caravans of bullock carts and pack-animals.
- Also, there were seafarers, whose ventures were risky but highly profitable.
- Successful merchants, designated as masattuvan in Tamil and setthis and satthavahas in Prakrit, could become enormously rich.
- A wide range of goods were carried from one place to another

- Spices, especially pepper, were in high demand in the Roman Empire, as were textiles and medicinal plants, and these were all transported across the Arabian Sea to the Mediterranean.

Coins and kings

- Punch-marked coins made of silver and copper (c. sixth century BCE onwards) were amongst the earliest to be minted and used.
- Numismatists have studied these and other coins to reconstruct possible commercial networks.
- The first coins to bear the names and images of rulers were issued by the Indo-Greeks, who established control over the north-western part of the subcontinent c. second century BCE.
- The kushanas, however, issued the largest hoards of gold coins first gold coins c. first century CE.
- Coins (Copper coins)were also issued by tribal republics such as that of the Yaudheyas of Punjab and Haryana (c. first century CE).
- Some of the most spectacular gold coins were issued by the Gupta rulers.
- From c. sixth century CE onwards, finds of gold coins taper off.

Terminologies

Periplus

- "Periplus" is a Greek word meaning sailing around and "Erythraean" was the Greek name for the Red Sea

Numismatics

- It is the study of coins, including visual elements such as scripts and images, metallurgical analysis and the contexts in which they have been found.

Back to Basics

Deciphering Brahmi

- Most scripts used to write modern Indian languages are derived from Brahmi, the script used in most Asokan inscriptions.
- Scholars who studied early inscriptions sometimes assumed these were in Sanskrit, although the earliest inscriptions were, in fact, in Prakrit.
- James Prinsep was able to decipher Asokan Brahmi in 1838.

Decipherment of Kharosthi

- The coins of Indo-Greek kings contain the names of kings written in Greek and Kharosthi scripts.
- With Prinsep identifying the language of the Kharosthi inscriptions as Prakrit, it became possible to read longer inscriptions as well.

Exercise

Level - 1

1. Rigveda was composed by people living along which of the following rivers?

(a) Indus (b) Ganga

(c) Kaveri (d) Godavari

2. James Prinsep, deciphered which of the following inscriptions?

(a) Brahmi (b) Kharosthi

(c) Khmer inscriptions (d) Both 1 and 2

3. Most of inscriptions mentioned a king referred to as _

(a) Piyadassi (b) Krishnasarah

(c) Devanampriya (d) Rajkiye

4. The earliest inscriptions were written in which of the following languages?

(a) Prakrit (b) Pali

(c) Sanskrit (d) Brahmi

5. Which of the following rulers was known from Prakrit texts and inscriptions

(a) Ajatasattu (b) Asoka

(c) Chandragupt Maurya (d) Both a and b

6. Janapada means the land where

(a) People settles

(b) King settles

(c) Jansabha called by the king

(d) None of the above

7. Ganas or Sanghas, were oligarchies, where power was shared by a number of men, often collectively called

(a) Rajas (b) Janas

(c) Brahmanas (d) Kshatriyas

8. Sanskrit texts Dharmasutras were composed by which of the following communities?

(a) Brahmanas (b) Kshatriyas

(c) Kautilya (d) Vaishyas

9. Which of the following languages was used to write inscriptions and texts.

(a) Pali (b) Tamil

(c) Sanskrit (d) all of the three

10. Magadha became the most powerful mahajanapada in which of the following periods?

(a) Between the sixth and the fourth centuries

(b) Between the second and the fourth centuries

(c) Between the first and the third centuries

(d) Between the fifth and the sixth centuries

11. Which of the following is not the king of Magadh ?

(a) Bimbisara (b) **Bindusara**

(c) Ajatasattu (d) Mahapadma Nanda

12. Most of the Asokan inscriptions are in which of the following languages?

(a) Prakrit (b) Aramaic and Greek

(c) Brahmi (d) Both a and c

13. The Aramaic and Greek scripts were used for inscriptions in which of the following countries?

(a) Sri Lanka (b) Bhutan

(c) Afghanistan (d) Vietnam

14. Megasthenes was a Greek ambassador to the court of which of the following rulers?

(a) Chandragupta Maurya

(b) Samundragupta Maurya

(c) Dhana Nanda

(d) Bindusara

15. Arthashastra has been composed by which of the following authors?

(a) Chanakya

(b) Harshvardhan

(c) Chandragupta Maurya

(d) None of the above

16. Who was the first ruler who inscribed his messages to his subjects and officials on stone surfaces?

(a) Samundragupta (b) Asoka

(c) Indo-greek (d) Pushyamitra Shunga

17. The Prayaga Prashasti was composed in Sanskrit by Harishena, the court poet of which of the following rulers?

(a) Chandragupta Maurya

(b) Samudragupta

(c) DhanaNanda

(d) Ashoka

18. Find the incorrect statement about Sudarshana lake

(a) The lake, was built by a local governor during the rule of the Mauryas

(b) It was repaired twice by Gupta dynasty.

(c) It was an artificial reservoir.

(d) The lake is situated in Gujrat

19. A gahapati was the owner, master or head of which of the following?

(a) Village (b) Household

(c) Sadar (d) Gram

20. Manusmrti is one of the best-known legal texts of early India, written in which of the following languages?

    (a) Sanskrit

    (b) Prakrit

    (c) Brahmi

    (d) Devnagri

21. An *agrahara* was land granted to

    (a) King

    (b) Zamindars

    (c) Brahmana

    (d) Local People

Level - 2

22. Find the False statement with respect to the developments after the end of the Harappan civilisation

    (a) The dead were buried with a rich range of iron tools and weapons.

    (b) Evidence of pastoral populations in the North

    (c) Making of elaborate stone structures known as megaliths

    (d) Emergence of early states, empires and kingdoms.

23. Find the true statements about Inscriptions

    (a) Inscriptions are virtually permanent records

    (b) Inscriptions are writings engraved on stones only

    (c) Inscriptions usually mentions the record of agriculture and tax activities

    (d) Both a and b

24. Find the false statement about mahajanapadas

    (a) Most mahajanapadas were ruled by single king

    (b) Each mahajanapada had a capital city

    (c) The capital city was often fortified

    (d) Both Buddhist and Jaina texts mention, sixteen states known as mahajanapadas.

25. Find the true statement about Magadha

    (a) Horse was the important component of the army

    (b) Rajagaha was the capital of Magadha

    (c) Rajagaha was a fortified settlement, located near the alluvial plains of Ganga.

    (d) In the third century BCE, the capital was shifted to Pataliputra

Answers

Level-1

1. (a)	2. (d)	3. (a)	4. (a)	5. (d)	6. (a)	7. (a)	8. (a)	9. (d)	10. (a)
11. (b)	12. (a)	13. (c)	14. (a)	15. (a)	16. (b)	17. (b)	18. (b)	19. (b)	20. (a)
21. (c)									

Level-2

22. (b)	23. (a)	24. (a)	25. (b)

Explanations

Level - 1

1. a • Rigveda was composed by people living along the Indus and its tributaries.

2. d • James Prinsep, an officer in the mint of the East India Company, deciphered Brahmi and Kharosthi, two scripts used in the earliest inscriptions and coins.

3. a • Most of the inscription mentioned a king referred to as Piyadassi – meaning "pleasant to behold"

• There were a few inscriptions which also referred to the king as Asoka, one of the most famous rulers known from Buddhist texts.

4. a • The earliest inscriptions were in Prakrit, a name for languages used by ordinary people.

5. d • Ajatasattu and Asoka, known from Prakrit texts and inscriptions

6. a • Janapada means the land where a jana (a people, clan or tribe) sets its foot or settles. It is a word used in both Prakrit and Sanskrit.

7. a • Most mahajanapadas were ruled by kings, some, known as ganas or sanghas, were oligarchies, where power was shared by a number of men, often collectively called rajas.

8. a • From c. sixth century BCE onwards, Brahmanas began composing Sanskrit texts known as the Dharmasutras.

• These laid down norms for rulers (as well as for other social categories), who were ideally expected to be Kshatriyas

9. d • Pali, Tamil and Sanskrit, were also used to write inscriptions and texts.

10. a • Between the sixth and the fourth centuries BCE, Magadha (in present-day Bihar) became the most powerful mahajanapada.

11. b • Early Buddhist and Jaina writers who wrote about Magadha attributed its power to the policies of individuals: ruthlessly ambitious kings of whom Bimbisara, Ajatasattu and Mahapadma Nanda are the best known

12. a • Most Asokan inscriptions were in the Prakrit language while those in the northwest of the subcontinet were in Aramaic and Greek.

13. c • The Aramaic and Greek scripts were used for inscriptions in Afghanistan.

14. a • Megasthenes (a Greek ambassador to the court of Chandragupta Maurya)

15. a • The Arthashastra is an ancient Indian Sanskrit treatise on statecraft, economic policy and military strategy. Kautilya, also identified as Vishnugupta and Chanakya, is traditionally credited as the author of the text.

16. b • The inscriptions of Asoka (c. 272/268-231 BCE) on rocks and pillars

• Asoka was the first ruler who inscribed his messages to his subjects and officials on stone surfaces – natural rocks as well as polished pillars.

17. b • The Prayaga Prashasti (also known as the Allahabad Pillar Inscription) composed in Sanskrit by Harishena, the court poet of Samudragupta, arguably the most powerful of the Gupta rulers (c. fourth century CE)

18. b • The Sudarshana lake was an artificial reservoir.

• The inscription mentions that the lake, with embankments and water channels, was built by a local governor during the rule of the Mauryas.

• Rudradaman, repaired the lake using his own resources, without imposing any tax on his subjects.

• Another inscription on the same rock (c. fifth century) mentions how one of the rulers of the Gupta dynasty got the lake repaired once again.

19. b • A gahapati was the owner, master or head of a household, who exercised control over the women, children, slaves and workers who shared a common residence.

• He was also the owner of the resources – land, animals and other things – that belonged to the household.

20. a • It is one of the best-known legal texts of early India, written in Sanskrit and compiled between c. second century BCE and c. second century CE.

21. c • An *agrahara* was land granted to a Brahmana, who was usually exempted from paying land revenue and other dues to the king, and was often given the right to collect these dues from the local people.

<u>Level - 2</u>

22. b Developments after the end of the Harappan civilisation.

- Evidence of pastoral populations in the Deccan and further south.
- New modes of disposal of the dead, including the making of elaborate stone structures known as megaliths, emerged in central and south India from the first millennium BCE.
- In many cases, the dead were buried with a rich range of iron tools and weapons.
- emergence of early states, empires and kingdoms.

23. a Inscriptions

- Inscriptions are writings engraved on hard surfaces such as stone, metal or pottery.
- They usually record the achievements, activities or ideas of those who commissioned them
- It includes the exploits of kings, or donations made by women and men to religious institutions.

- Inscriptions are virtually permanent records, some of which carry dates.

24. a
- Early Buddhist and Jaina texts mention, amongst other things, sixteen states known as mahajanapadas.
- Most mahajanapadas were ruled by kings, some, known as ganas or sanghas, were oligarchies, where power was shared by a number of men, often collectively called rajas.
- Each mahajanapada had a capital city, which was often fortified

25. b
- Elephants, an important component of the army, were found in forests in the region.
- Initially, Rajagaha (the Prakrit name for present-day Rajgir in Bihar) was the capital of Magadha.
- Rajagaha was a fortified settlement, located amongst hills.
- Later, in the fourth century BCE, the capital was shifted to Pataliputra, present-day Patna

CHAPTER 3

Kinship, Caste and Class

Early Societies (c. 600 BCE-600 CE)

1. The Critical Edition of the Mahabharata

- Prepared by (1919) - A team comprising dozens of scholars under the leadership of a noted Indian Sanskritist, V.S. Sukthankar
- Objective - Collecting Sanskrit manuscripts of the text, written in a variety of scripts, from different parts of the country.
- The project took 47 years to complete.

Two things became apparent

1. Several common elements in the Sanskrit versions of the story, evident in manuscripts found all over the subcontinent, from Kashmir and Nepal in the north to Kerala and Tamil Nadu in the south.
2. Enormous regional variations in the ways in which the text had been transmitted over the centuries.

Outcome

- Our understanding of these processes is derived primarily from texts written in Sanskrit by and for Brahmanas.
- Everything that was laid down in these texts was not actually practised.
- The ideas contained in normative Sanskrit texts were on the whole recognised as authoritative
- They were also questioned and occasionally even rejected.

The *Mahabharata*

- A colossal epic running in its present form into over 100,000 verses with depictions of a wide range of social categories and situations
- It was composed over a period of about 1,000 years (*c.* 500 BCE onwards)
- The Mahabharata describes a feud over land and power between two groups of cousins, the Kauravas and the Pandavas, who belonged to a single ruling family, that of the Kurus, a lineage dominating one of the janapadas

- Ultimately, the conflict ended in a battle, in which the Pandavas emerged victorious.
- After that, patrilineal succession was proclaimed

2. Kinship and Marriage : Many Rules and Varied Practices

Ideal of patriliny

- Under patriliny, sons could claim the resources (including the throne in the case of kings) of their fathers when the latter died.
- Most ruling dynasties (c. sixth century BCE onwards) claimed to follow this system
- The patriliny had existed prior to the composition of the epic
- *Mahabharata* reinforced the idea that it was valuable.

Rules of marriage

- Sons were important for the continuity of the patrilineage, daughters were viewed rather differently within this framework.
- Daughters had no claims to the resources of the household.
- Marrying them into families outside the kin was considered desirable. This system, called exogamy

Codes of social behaviour

- The Brahmanas laid down the codes of social behaviour
- These were meant to be followed by Brahmanas in particular and the rest of society in general.
- From c. 500 BCE, these norms were compiled in Sanskrit texts known as the Dharmasutras and Dharmashastras.
- The most important of such works, the Manusmriti, was compiled between c. 200 BCE and 200 CE.
- The influence of Brahmanas was by no means all-pervasive.

- The Dharmasutras and Dharmashastras recognised as many as eight forms of marriage.
- Of these, the first four were considered as "good" while the remaining were condemned.
- It is possible that these were practised by those who did not accept Brahmanical norms.

The gotra of women

- Brahmanical practice(from c. 1000 BCE onwards was to classify people (especially Brahmanas) in terms of gotras.
- Each gotra was named after a Vedic seer, and all those who belonged to the same gotra were regarded as his descendants.
- Two rules about gotra were particularly important: women were expected to give up their father's gotra and adopt that of their husband on marriage and members of the same gotra could not marry.

Terminologies

- *Patriliny* means tracing descent from father to son, grandson and so on.

  Matriliny is the term used when descent is traced through the mother
- Sanskrit texts use the term kula to designate families and jnati for the larger network of kinfolk.
- The term vamsha is used for lineage
- Endogamy refers to marriage within a unit – this could be a kin group, caste, or a group living in the same locality.
- Exogamy refers to marriage outside the unit.
- Polygyny is the practice of a man having several wives.
- Polyandry is the practice of a woman having several husbands.

3. Social Differences: Within and Beyond the Framework of Caste

- Caste - set of hierarchically ordered social categories.
- The ideal order was laid down in the Dharmasutras and Dharmashastras.
- Brahmanas - ranked first
- Shudras and "untouchables" at the very bottom of the social order.
- Positions within the order were supposedly determined by birth.

The "right" occupation

- The Dharmasutras and Dharmashastras also contained rules about the ideal "occupations" of the four categories or *varnas.*

- Brahmanas - to study and teach the Vedas, perform sacrifices and get sacrifices performed, and give and receive gifts.
- Kshatriyas -to engage in warfare, protect people and administer justice, study the Vedas, get sacrifices performed, and make gifts.
- The last three "occupations" were assigned to the Vaishyas, who were in addition expected to engage in agriculture, pastoralism and trade.
- Shudras were assigned only one occupation – that of serving the three "higher" *varnas.*

Non-Kshatriya kings

- According to the Shastras, only Kshatriyas could be kings.

Debatable

- The later Buddhist texts suggested that the Mauryas were Kshatriyas, Brahmanical texts described them as being of "low" origin.
- The Shungas and Kanvas, the immediate successors of the Mauryas, were Brahmanas.
- Other rulers, such as the Shakas who came from Central Asia, were regarded as mlechchhas, barbarians or outsiders by the Brahmanas.
- The Satavahana dynasty, Gotami-puta Siri-Satakani, claimed to be both a unique Brahmana and a destroyer of the pride of Kshatriyas.
- He also claimed to have ensured that there was no intermarriage amongst members of the four varnas. At the same time, he entered into a marriage alliance with the kin of Rudradaman.

Jatis and social mobility

- In Brahmanical theory, jati, like varna, was based on birth.
- However, while the number of varnas was fixed at four, there was no restriction on the number of jatis.
- In fact, whenever Brahmanical authorities encountered new groups – for instance, people living in forests such as the nishadas – or wanted to assign a name to occupational categories such as the goldsmith or suvarnakara, which did not easily fit into the fourfold varna system, they classified them as a jati.
- Jatis which shared a common occupation or profession were sometimes organised into shrenis or guilds.

Beyond the four *varnas*: Integration

- Categories such as the *nishada* were not influenced by Brahmanical ideas
- They are often described as odd, uncivilised, or even animal-like.

- Brahmanas considered them outside the system
- Others who were viewed with suspicion included populations such as nomadic pastoralists
- Sometimes those who spoke non-Sanskritic languages were labelled as *mlechchhas* and looked down upon.

Beyond the four *varnas* Subordination and conflict

- Brahmanas also developed a sharper social divide by classifying certain social categories as "untouchable".
- Some activities were regarded as particularly "polluting". These included handling corpses and dead animals.
- Those who performed such tasks, designated as *chandalas,* were placed at the very bottom of the hierarchy.
- The *Manusmriti* laid down the "duties" of the *chandalas.*
- The Chinese Buddhist monk Fa Xian (*c.* fifth century CE) and a Chinese pilgrim, Xuan Zang (*c.* seventh century) wrote about untouchables.

4. Beyond Birth Resources and Status

Gendered access to property

- According to the *Manusmriti,* the paternal estate was to be divided equally amongst sons after the death of the parents, with a special share for the eldest.
- Women could not claim a share of these resources.
- However, women were allowed to retain the gifts they received on the occasion of their marriage as *stridhana*
- This could be inherited by their children, without the husband having any claim on it.

- At the same time, the *Manusmriti* warned women against hoarding family property, or even their own valuables, without the husband's permission.
- For men, the Manusmriti declares, there are seven means of acquiring wealth: inheritance, finding, purchase, conquest, investment, work, and acceptance of gifts from good people.
- For women, there are six means of acquiring wealth: what was given in front of the fire (marriage) or the bridal procession, or as a token of affection, and what she got from her brother, mother or father.
- She could also acquire wealth through any subsequent gift and whatever her "affectionate" husband might give her.

***Varna* and access to property**

- According to the Brahmanical texts, another criterion (apart from gender) for regulating access to wealth was *varna.*
- The only "occupation" prescribed for Shudras was servitude, while a variety of occupations were listed for men of the first three *varnas.*
- If these provisions were actually implemented, the wealthiest men would have been the Brahmanas and the Kshatriyas.
- Even as the Brahmanical view of society was codified in the Dharmasutras and Dharmashastras, other traditions developed critiques of the *varna* order.
- The Buddhists recognised that there were differences in society, but did not regard these as natural or inflexible.
- They also rejected the idea of claims to status on the basis of birth.

Exercise

Level - 1

1. From which of the following regions did the Shakas come to India?

   (a) Central Asia   (b) Egypt

   (c) South East Asia   (d) Mongolia

2. The Brihadaranyaka Upanishad, one of the early Upanishads, contains a list of successive generations of _

   (a) Teachers and Students

   (b) Priests and Kings

   (c) Monks and Preachers

   (d) None of the above

3. Most ruling dynasties claimed to follow the system of patriliny from _

   (a) Sixth century BCE onwards

   (b) Fifth century BCE onwards

   (c) Second century BCE onwards

   (d) Third century BCE onwards

4. Endogamy refers to marriage within a _

   (a) Caste   (b) Community

   (c) Unit   (d) Both a and b

5. Find out the correct statement with reference to the rules of marriage

   (a) Sons and daughters both were important for the continuity of the patrilineage/Matrilineage

   (b) Daughters had equal claim on the resources of the household.

   (c) Marrying daughters into families outside the kin was considered desirable

   (d) All of the above

6. Exogamy refers to marriage _

   (a) outside the unit.

   (b) within a unit

   (c) within designated families

   (d) outsider the territory

7. Polygyny is the practice of

   (a) a man having several wives.

   (b) a woman having several husbands.

   (c) a man having wife outside the unit

   (d) a woman having husband outside the unit

8. Find the incorrect statement

   (a) Polyandry is the practice of a woman having several husbands.

   (b) *Patriliny* means tracing descent from father to son, grandson and so on.

   (c) *Matriliny* is the term used when descent is traced through the mother

   (d) None of the above

9. The term vamsha was used for

   (a) Family lineage   (b) social behaviour

   (c) patrilineage   (d) janapadas

10. The code of social behaviour was determined by which of the following social categories?

    (a) Brahmanas   (b) Kshatriyas

    (c) Vaishyas   (d) Both (a) and (b)

11. The codes of social behaviour were compiled in Sanskrit texts and referred as

    (a) Dharmasutras   (b) Dharmashastras.

    (c) Vedic seer   (d) Both a and b

12. Later Buddhist texts suggested that the Mauryas were

    (a) Brahmanas

    (b) Kshatriyas

    (c) Mlechchhas

    (d) Barbarians or outsiders

13. Which of the following was not the profession of Brahmins?

    (a) study and teach the Vedas

    (b) perform sacrifices

    (c) administer justice

    (d) give and receive gifts.

14. Mlechhas are people who speak which of the following languages

    (a) Non-Sanskritic languages

    (b) Sanskritic languages

    (c) Parakit Language

    (d) Indo- Greek Language

15. The duties of the *chandalas had been mentioned in which of the following texts?*

    (a) Dharmasutras   (b) Dharmashastras

    (c) Manusmriti   (d) Mlechchhas

16. The Chinese Buddhist monk Fa Xian and a Chinese pilgrim, Xuan Zang wrote about which of the following subjects?

    (a) Untouchability   (b) Buddhism

    (c) Varnas   (d) Jatis

Level - 2

17. Which of the following statement is false regarding the Ideal of patriliny

    (a) The patriliny had existed prior to the composition of Mahabharata

    (b) *Mahabharata* reinforced the idea of patriliny

    (c) Most ruling dynasties claimed to follow this system

    (d) Patrilineal succession was abolished after the conclusion of Mahabharata battle

18. Find the true statements about the epic *Mahabharata*

    (a) It was composed over a period of about 500 years

    (b) The conflict ended in a battle, in which the Kurus emerged victorious

    (c) Kauravas and the Pandavas, belonged to a single ruling family

    (d) Patrilineal succession was abolished after the battle

19. Find the correct statement about Dharmasutras and Dharmashastras.

    (a) It recognised as many as eight forms of marriage.

    (b) All marriages were considered as good

    (c) The forms of marriage were practised only by those who accept Brahmanical norms.

    (d) None of the above

20. Which of the following is true about gotras.

    (a) Each gotra was named after a Vedic seer

    (b) Women were expected to carry their father's gotra after marriage

    (c) Members of the same gotra can marry under exceptional circumstances

    (d) All of the above

21. The hierarchically ordered social categories of castes were supposedly determined by

    (a) birth

    (b) Occupation

    (c) varnas

    (d) gotra

22. Find the correct statement:

    (a) The Shungas and Kanvas, were the immediate successors of the Mauryas

    (b) The Shungas and Kanvas were Brahmanas.

    (c) The Shakas came from Central Asia

    (d) All of the above

23. Find the incorrect statement about Jatis

    (a) There were certain restriction on the number of jatis.

    (b) It was based on birth.

    (c) Jatis were sometimes organised into shrenis or guilds.

    (d) None of the above

Answers

Level-1

1. (a)	2. (a)	3. (a)	4. (c)	5. (c)	6. (a)	7. (a)	8. (d)	9. (a)	10. (a)
11. (d)	12. (b)	13. (c)	14. (a)	15. (c)	16. (a)				

Level-2

17. (d)	18. (c)	19. (a)	20. (a)	21. (a)	22. (d)	23. (a)

Explanations

Level - 1

1. a • Rulers, such as the Shakas who came from Central Asia, were regarded as mlechchhas, barbarians or outsiders by the Brahmanas

2. a • The Brihadaranyaka Upanishad, one of the earliest Upanishads contains a list of successive generations of teachers and students, many of whom were designated by metronymics.

3. a • Under patriliny, sons could claim the resources (including the throne in the case of kings) of their fathers when the latter died.
 • Most ruling dynasties (c. sixth century BCE onwards) claimed to follow this system

4. c • Endogamy refers to marriage within a unit – this could be a kin group, caste, or a group living in the same locality.

5. c • Sons were important for the continuity of the patrilineage, daughters were viewed rather differently within this framework.
 • Daughters had no claims to the resources of the household.
 • Marrying them into families outside the kin was considered desirable

6. a • Exogamy refers to marriage outside the unit.

7. a • Polygyny is the practice of a man having several wives.

8. d • *Patriliny* means tracing descent from father to son, grandson and so on.
 • *Matriliny* is the term used when descent is traced through the mother
 • Polyandry is the practice of a woman having several husbands.

9. a • The term vamsha is a Sanskrit word that means 'family, lineage'

10. a • The Brahmanas laid down the codes of social behaviour

11. d • From c. 500 BCE, these norms (codes of social behaviour) were compiled in Sanskrit texts known as the Dharmasutras and Dharmashastras.

12. b • The later Buddhist texts suggested that the Mauryas were Kshatriyas, Brahmanical texts described them as being of "low" origin.

13. c • Brahmanas - to study and teach the Vedas, perform sacrifices and get sacrifices performed, and give and receive gifts.

14. a • Those who spoke non-Sanskritic languages were labelled as *mlechchhas* and looked down upon.

15. c • The *Manusmriti* laid down the "duties" of the *chandalas*.

16. a • The Chinese Buddhist monk Fa Xian (*c.* fifth century CE) and a Chinese pilgrim, Xuan Zang (*c.* seventh century) wrote about untouchables

Level - 2

17. d • Under patriliny, sons could claim the resources (including the throne in the case of kings) of their fathers when the latter died.
 • Most ruling dynasties (c. sixth century BCE onwards) claimed to follow this system
 • The patriliny had existed prior to the composition of the epic
 • *Mahabharata* reinforced the idea that it was valuable.

18. c • It was composed over a period of about 1,000 years (*c.* 500 BCE onwards)
 • The Mahabharata describes a feud over land and power between two groups of cousins, the Kauravas and the Pandavas, who belonged to a single ruling family, that of the Kurus, a lineage dominating one of the janapadas
 • After that, patrilineal succession was proclaimed

19. a • The Dharmasutras and Dharmashastras recognised as many as eight forms of marriage.
 • Of these, the first four were considered as "good" while the remaining were condemned.
 • It is possible that these were practised by those who did not accept Brahmanical norms.

20. a • Brahmanical practice (from c. 1000 BCE onwards was to classify people (especially Brahmanas) in terms of gotras.
 • Each gotra was named after a Vedic seer, and all those who belonged to the same gotra were regarded as his descendants.
 • Two rules about gotra were particularly important: women were expected to give up their father's gotra and adopt that of their husband on marriage and members of the same gotra could not marry.

21. a • Positions within the order were supposedly determined by birth.

22. d • The Shungas and Kanvas, the immediate successors of the Mauryas, were Brahmanas.
 • The Shakas came from Central Asia, were regarded as outsiders by the Brahmanas.

23. a • It was based on birth.
 • However, while the number of varnas was fixed at four, there was no restriction on the number of jatis.
 • Jatis which shared a common occupation or profession were sometimes organised into shrenis or guilds.

CHAPTER 4

THEME FOUR

Thinkers, Beliefs and Buildings

Cultural Developments (c. 600 BCE-600 CE)

1. A Glimpse of Sanchi

Stupa at Sanchi.

- One of the most important Buddhist centres
- The discovery of Sanchi has vastly transformed our understanding of early Buddhism.
- The rulers of Bhopal, Shahjehan Begum and her successor Sultan Jehan Begum, provided money for the preservation of the ancient site.

2. The Background

Mid-first millennium BCE

- Turning point in world history
- Emergence of thinkers such as Zarathustra in Iran, Kong Zi in China, Socrates, Plato and Aristotle in Greece, and Mahavira and Gautama Buddha in India.

The sacrificial tradition

- Several pre-existing traditions of thought, religious belief and practice, including the early Vedic tradition, known from the *Rigveda*, compiled between c.1500 and 1000 BCE.
- The *Rigveda* consists of hymns in praise of a variety of deities, especially Agni, Indra and Soma.
- Many of these hymns were chanted when sacrifices were performed, where people prayed for cattle, sons, good health, long life, etc.
- At first, sacrifices were performed collectively.
- Later (c. 1000 BCE-500 BCE onwards) some were performed by the heads of households for the well-being of the domestic unit.
- More elaborate sacrifices, such as the *rajasuya* and *ashvamedha*, were performed by chiefs and kings who depended on Brahmana priests to conduct the ritual.

How Buddhist texts were prepared and preserved

- The Buddha (and other teachers) taught orally – through discussion and debate.
- None of the Buddha's speeches were written down during his lifetime.
- After his death (c. fifth-fourth century BCE) his teachings were compiled by his disciples at a council of "elders" or senior monks at Vesali (Pali for Vaishali in present-day Bihar).
- These compilations were known as Tipitaka – literally, three baskets to hold different types of texts.
- The Vinaya Pitaka included rules and regulations for those who joined the sangha or monastic order
- The Buddha's teachings were included in the Sutta Pitaka
- The Abhidhamma Pitaka dealt with philosophical matters.
- Each pitaka comprised a number of individual texts.
- Later, commentaries were written on these texts by Buddhist scholars.
- Other texts such as the Dipavamsa (literally, the chronicle of the island) and Mahavamsa (the great chronicle) were written, containing regional histories of Buddhism.

3. Beyond Worldly Pleasures

The Message of Mahavira

- Mahavira was preceded by 23 other teachers or *tirthankaras*
- The most important idea in Jainism is that the entire world is animated: even stones, rocks and water have life.
- Non-injury to living beings, especially to humans, animals, plants and insects, is central to Jaina philosophy.
- According to Jaina teachings, the cycle of birth and rebirth is shaped through karma.
- Asceticism and penance are required to free oneself from the cycle of karma.

- This can be achieved only by renouncing the world; therefore, monastic existence is a necessary condition of salvation.
- Jaina monks and nuns took five vows: to abstain from killing, stealing and lying; to observe celibacy; and to abstain from possessing property.

4. The Buddha and the Quest for Enlightenment

- Siddhartha, as the Buddha was named at birth, was the son of a chief of the Sakya clan.
- He had a sheltered upbringing within the palace, insulated from the harsh realities of life. One day he persuaded his charioteer to take him into the city.
- His first journey into the world outside was traumatic.
- He was deeply anguished when he saw an old man, a sick man and a corpse.
- He realised in that moment that the decay and destruction of the human body was inevitable.
- He also saw a homeless mendicant, who, it seemed to him, had come to terms with old age, disease and death, and found peace.
- Siddhartha decided that he too would adopt the same path.
- Soon after, he left the palace and set out in search of his own truth.
- Siddhartha explored several paths including bodily mortification which led him to a situation of near death.
- Abandoning these extreme methods, he meditated for several days and finally attained enlightenment.
- After this he came to be known as the Buddha or the Enlightened One.
- For the rest of his life, he taught dhamma or the path of righteous living.
- Buddha's message spread across the subcontinent and beyond – through Central Asia to China, Korea and Japan, and through Sri Lanka, across the seas to Myanmar, Thailand and Indonesia.

5. The Teachings of the Buddha

- The Buddha's teachings have been reconstructed from stories, found mainly in the Sutta Pitaka.
- According to Buddhist philosophy, the world is transient (anicca) and constantly changing; it is also soulless (anatta) as there is nothing permanent or eternal in it.
- Within this transient world, sorrow (dukkha) is intrinsic to human existence.
- It is by following the path of moderation between severe penance and self-indulgence that human beings can rise above these worldly troubles.

- In the earliest forms of Buddhism, whether or not god existed was irrelevant.
- The Buddha regarded the social world as the creation of humans rather than of divine origin.

6. Followers of the Buddha

- Buddha founded a sangha, an organisation of monks who too became teachers of dhamma. These monks lived simply, possessing only the essential requisites for survival
- As they lived on alms, they were known as bhikkhus.
- Initially, only men were allowed into the sangha, but later women also came to be admitted. This was made possible through the mediation of Ananda, one of the Buddha's dearest disciples, who persuaded him to allow women into the sangha.
- The Buddha's foster mother, Mahapajapati Gotami was the first woman to be ordained as a bhikkhuni.
- The Buddha's followers were regarded as equal, having shed their earlier social identities on becoming bhikkhus and bhikkhunis.
- The internal functioning of the sangha was based on the traditions of ganas and sanghas, where consensus was arrived at through discussions.

The Therigatha

- This unique Buddhist text, part of the Sutta Pitaka, is a collection of verses composed by bhikkhunis.
- It provides an insight into women's social and spiritual experiences.

7. Stupas

- From earliest times, people tended to regard certain places as sacred.
- These included sites with special trees or unique rocks, or sites of awe-inspiring natural beauty.
- These sites, with small shrines attached to them, were sometimes described as chaityas.
- Buddhist literature mentions several chaityas.
- It also describes places associated with the Buddha's life – where he was born (Lumbini), where he attained enlightenment (Bodh Gaya), where he gave his first sermon (Sarnath) and where he attained nibbana (Kusinagara).
- Gradually, each of these places came to be regarded as sacred.
- About 200 years after the time of the Buddha, Asoka erected a pillar at Lumbini to mark the fact that he had visited the place.

About Stupas

- Relics of the Buddha such as his bodily remains or objects used by him were buried there.

- These were mounds known as stupas.
- The tradition of erecting stupas may have been pre-Buddhist, but they came to be associated with Buddhism.
- According to a Buddhist text known as the Ashokavadana, Asoka distributed portions of the Buddha's relics to every important town and ordered the construction of stupas over them.(eg Bharhut, Sanchi and Sarnath)

How were stupas built

- donations made by kings such as the Satavahanas
- donations were made by guilds (eg. ivory workers who financed part of one of the gateways at Sanchi)
- Bhikkhus and bhikkhunis also contributed towards building these monuments.

The structure of the stupa

- The stupa (a Sanskrit word meaning a heap) originated as a simple semi-circular mound of earth, later called anda.
- Gradually, it evolved into a more complex structure, balancing round and square shapes.
- Above the anda was the harmika, a balcony- like structure that represented the abode of the gods.
- Arising from the *harmika* was a mast called the *yashti*, often surmounted by a *chhatri* or umbrella.
- Around the mound was a railing, separating the sacred space from the secular world.

8. Amaravati and Sanchi Stupa

Why did Sanchi survive while Amaravati did not ?

- *in situ* preservation was not adopted for Amaravati but in the case of Sanchi, it was adopted by the British authorites
- Amaravati was discovered before scholars understood the value of the finds and realised how critical it was to preserve things where they had been found instead of removing them from the site.
- When Sanchi was "discovered" in 1818, three of its four gateways were still standing, the fourth was lying on the spot where it had fallen and the mound was in good condition

9. New Religious Traditions

The development of Mahayana Buddhism

- By the first century CE, there is evidence of changes in Buddhist ideas and practices.
- Early Buddhist teachings had given great importance to self-effort in achieving *nibbana*.
- Besides, the Buddha was regarded as a human being who attained enlightenment and *nibbana* through his own efforts.

- However, gradually the idea of a saviour emerged.
- It was believed that he was the one who could ensure salvation.
- Simultaneously, the concept of the Bodhisatta also developed.
- Bodhisattas were perceived as deeply compassionate beings who accumulated merit through their efforts but used this not to attain *nibbana* and thereby abandon the world, but to help others.
- The worship of images of the Buddha and Bodhisattas became an important part of this tradition.
- This new way of thinking was called Mahayana – literally, the "great vehicle".
- Those who adopted these beliefs described the older tradition as Hinayana or the "lesser vehicle".
- Supporters of Mahayana regarded other Buddhists as followers of Hinayana.
- However, followers of the older tradition described themselves as theravadins, that is, those who followed the path of old, respected teachers, the theras.

The growth of Puranic Hinduism

- The notion of a saviour was not unique to Buddhism.
- Similar ideas being developed in different ways within traditions that we now consider part of Hinduism.
- These included Vaishnavism (a form of Hinduism within which Vishnu was worshipped as the principal deity) and Shaivism (a tradition within which Shiva was regarded as the chief god), in which there was growing emphasis on the worship of a chosen deity.
- In such worship the bond between the devotee and the god was visualised as one of love and devotion, or bhakti.

Building temples

- The early temple was a small square room, called the garbhagriha, with a single doorway for the worshipper to enter and offer worship to the image.
- Gradually, a tall structure, known as the *shikhara*, was built over the central shrine.
- Temple walls were often decorated with sculpture.
- Later temples became far more elaborate – with assembly halls, huge walls and gateways, and arrangements for supplying water
- One of the unique features of early temples was that some of these were hollowed out of huge rocks, as artificial caves.
- The tradition of building artificial caves was an old one.
- Some of the earliest of these were constructed in the third century BCE on the orders of Asoka for renouncers who belonged to the Ajivika sect.

Exercise

Level - 1

1. Socrates, Plato and Aristotle were thinkers of which of the following countries?
   - (a) Greece
   - (b) Iran
   - (c) China
   - (d) Portuguese

2. The teachings of Buddha were compiled by one of his disciples who was known by the name of
   - (a) Vinaya Pitaka
   - (b) Sutta Pitaka
   - (c) Abhidhamma Pitaka
   - (d) Tipitaka

3. Several pre-existing traditions of thought, religious belief and practice, including the early Vedic tradition, were known from which of the following texts?
   - (a) Yajurveda
   - (b) *Rigveda*
   - (c) Upanishads
   - (d) *Tipitaka*

4. Rajasuya and *Ashvamedha* sacrifices were performed by who among the following ?
   - (a) Chiefs
   - (b) Kings
   - (c) Priests
   - (d) Both a and b

5. The Buddha and other teachers taught to their disciples _
   - (a) Through Vinaya Pitaka
   - (b) Through Sutta Pitaka
   - (c) Through debate and discussion
   - (d) through Written speeches of Buddha

6. About 200 years after the time of the Buddha, who among the following rulers erected a pillar at Lumbini to mark the fact that he had visited the place?
   - (a) Ashoka
   - (b) Chandragupt
   - (c) Samundragupt
   - (d) None of the above

7. Dipavamsa and Mahavamsa contain regional histories of which of the following religions?
   - (a) Buddhism
   - (b) Jainism
   - (c) Vaishnavism
   - (d) Shaivism

8. Gautam Buddha was deeply anguished when he saw which of the following events?
   - (a) an old man
   - (b) a sick man
   - (c) a corpse
   - (d) All of the above

9. The Buddha's teachings have been reconstructed from stories, found mainly in which of the following Pitakas
   - (a) Vinaya Pitaka
   - (b) Sutta Pitaka
   - (c) Abhidhamma Pitaka
   - (d) None of the above

10. The Therigatha is a collection of verses composed by
    - (a) Ananda
    - (b) Mahapajapati Gotami
    - (c) bhikkhus
    - (d) bhikkhunis

Level - 2

11. Find the incorrect statement about Sanchi Stupa
    - (a) British government provided money for the preservation of the ancient site.
    - (b) *In situ* preservation was not adopted for Sanchi Stupa
    - (c) It was one of the most important Buddhist centres
    - (d) It was discovered in 1818

12. The *Rigveda* consists of hymns in praise of which of the following deities?
    - (a) Agni
    - (b) Indra
    - (c) Soma
    - (d) All of the above

13. Find the correct statement about sacrifices
    - (a) Sacrifices were performed collectively in all periods
    - (b) Hymns were chanted when sacrifices were performed
    - (c) In Sacrifices people prayed for wealth and marriages
    - (d) None of the above

14. Jaina monks and nuns took which of the following vows:
    1. Abstain from killing   2. stealing
    3. lying   4. observe celibacy
    5. abstain from possessing property.

    Choose the correct answer from the codes given below
    - (a) 1, 3, 4 and 5
    - (b) 2, 3, 4 and 5
    - (c) 1, 3, 4 and 5
    - (d) 1, 2, 3, 4 and 5

15. Which of the following statement does not come under Jaina philosophy or teachings?
    - (a) Non-injury to living and non living being, is central to Jaina philosophy.
    - (b) The cycle of birth and rebirth is shaped through karma.
    - (c) Asceticism and penance are required to free oneself from the cycle of karma.
    - (d) Monastic existence is a necessary condition of salvation in Jainism

16. Find the incorrect statement about Pitaka

 (a) The Vinaya Pitaka included rules and regulations for those who joined the monastic order

 (b) Buddha's teachings were included in the Sutta Pitaka

 (c) The Abhidhamma Pitaka dealt with philosophical matters.

 (d) Each pitaka comprised a number discussions and debates.

17. Find the False statement about Buddha's sangha

 (a) It was an organisation of monks who too became teachers of dhamma.

 (b) Monks were known as bhikkhus and bhikkhunis.

 (c) Both men and Women were allowed into the sangha

 (d) Buddha's mother who gave him birth, Mahapajapati Gotami, was the first bhikkhuni.

18. From earliest times, people tended to regard certain places as sacred which include sites with special trees or unique rocks, with small shrines attached to them. These were sometimes described as _

 (a) Chaityas

 (b) Viharas

 (c) Sangha

 (d) Aalayam

19. Which of the following is not the place associated with the Buddha's life

 (a) Bodh Gaya   (b) Sarnath

 (c) Kusinagara   (d) Vaishali

20. Find the correct statement about Stupas

 (a) Relics of the Buddha were buried there.

 (b) The stupa originated as a simple semi-circular mound of earth

 (c) The tradition of erecting stupas started with Buddhism.

 (d) a and b only

21. Ashokavadana text belongs to which of the following religions?

 (a) Buddhism   (b) Hinduism

 (c) Vaishnavism   (d) Shaivism

22. Which of the following group of people contributed towards building stupas

 (a) Bhikkhus and bhikkhunis

 (b) Guilds

 (c) Kings

 (d) All of the above

23. In the structure of the stupa, harmika represents

 (a) abode of the gods   (b) umbrella.

 (c) secular world   (d) balancing shapes.

Answers

Level-1

 1. (a)   **2.** (d)   **3.** (b)   **4.** (d)   **5.** (d)   **6.** (a)   **7.** (a)   **8.** (d)   **9.** (b)   **10.** (c)

Level-2

 11. (a)   **12.** (d)   **13.** (b)   **14.** (d)   **15.** (a)   **16.** (d)   **17.** (d)   **18.** (a)   **19.** (d)   **20.** (d)

 21. (a)   **22.** (d)   **23.** (a)

Explanations

<table>
<tr><td valign="top">

Level - 1

1. a
- Mid-first millennium BCE was the turning point in world history where we saw emergence of thinkers such as Zarathustra in Iran, Kong Zi in China, Socrates, Plato and Aristotle in Greece, and Mahavira and Gautama Buddha in India.

2. d
- After his death (c. fifth-fourth century BCE) his teachings were compiled by his disciples at a council of "elders" or senior monks at Vesali (Pali for Vaishali in present-day Bihar).
- These compilations were known as Tipitaka – literally, three baskets to hold different types of texts.

3. b
- Several pre-existing traditions of thought, religious belief and practice, including the early Vedic tradition, known from the *Rigveda*, compiled between *c.*1500 and 1000 BCE.

4. d
- More elaborate sacrifices, such as the *rajasuya* and *ashvamedha*, were performed by chiefs and kings who depended on Brahmana priests to conduct the ritual.

5. d
- The Buddha (and other teachers) taught orally – through discussion and debate.
- None of the Buddha's speeches were written down during his lifetime.

6. a
- About 200 years after the time of the Buddha, Asoka erected a pillar at Lumbini to mark the fact that he had visited the place.

7. a
- Other texts such as the Dipavamsa (literally, the chronicle of the island) and Mahavamsa (the great chronicle) were written, containing regional histories of Buddhism.

8. d
- Siddhartha, as the Buddha was named at birth, was the son of a chief of the Sakya clan.
- He was deeply anguished when he saw an old man, a sick man and a corpse.

9. b
- The Buddha's teachings have been reconstructed from stories, found mainly in the Sutta Pitaka.

10. c
- It is a unique Buddhist text, part of the Sutta Pitaka, is a collection of verses composed by bhikkhunis.
- It provides an insight into women's social and spiritual experiences.

</td><td valign="top">

Level - 2

11. a
- The discovery of Sanchi has vastly transformed our understanding of early Buddhism.
- The rulers of Bhopal, Shahjehan Begum and her successor Sultan Jehan Begum, provided money for the preservation of the ancient site.

12. d
- The *Rigveda* consists of hymns in praise of a variety of deities, especially Agni, Indra and Soma.

13. b
- Many of these hymns were chanted when sacrifices were performed, where people prayed for cattle, sons, good health, long life, etc.
- At first, sacrifices were performed collectively.
- Later (*c.* 1000 BCE-500 BCE onwards) some were performed by the heads of households for the well- being of the domestic unit.

14. d
- Jaina monks and nuns took five vows: to abstain from killing, stealing and lying; to observe celibacy; and to abstain from possessing property.

15. a
- Non-injury to living beings, especially to humans, animals, plants and insects, is central to Jaina philosophy.
- According to Jaina teachings, the cycle of birth and rebirth is shaped through karma.
- Asceticism and penance are required to free oneself from the cycle of karma.
- This can be achieved only by renouncing the world; therefore, monastic existence is a necessary condition of salvation.

16. d
- The Vinaya Pitaka included rules and regulations for those who joined the sangha or monastic order
- The Buddha's teachings were included in the Sutta Pitaka
- The Abhidhamma Pitaka dealt with philosophical matters.
- Each pitaka comprised a number of individual texts.

17. d
- Buddha founded a sangha, an organisation of monks who too became teachers of dhamma.
- As they lived on alms, they were known as bhikkhus.
- Initially, only men were allowed into the sangha, but later women also came to be admitted.

</td></tr>
</table>

- The Buddha's foster mother, Mahapajapati Gotami was the first woman to be ordained as a bhikkhuni.

18. a
- From earliest times, people tended to regard certain places as sacred.
- These included sites with special trees or unique rocks, or sites of awe- inspiring natural beauty.
- These sites, with small shrines attached to them, were sometimes described as chaityas.

19. d
- Places associated with the Buddha's life – where he was born (Lumbini), where he attained enlightenment (Bodh Gaya), where he gave his first sermon (Sarnath) and where he attained nibbana (Kusinagara).

20. d
- Relics of the Buddha such as his bodily remains or objects used by him were buried there.
- These were mounds known as stupas.
- The tradition of erecting stupas may have been pre-Buddhist, but they came to be associated with Buddhism.

21. a
- According to a Buddhist text known as the Ashokavadana, Asoka distributed portions of the Buddha's relics to every important town and ordered the construction of stupas over them.(eg Bharhut, Sanchi and Sarnath)

22. d Stupas were built by
- donations made by kings such as the Satavahanas
- donations were made by guilds (eg. ivory workers who financed part of one of the gateways at Sanchi)
- Bhikkhus and bhikkhunis also contributed towards building these monuments.

23. a
- The stupa (a Sanskrit word meaning a heap) originated as a simple semi-circular mound of earth, later called anda.
- Gradually, it evolved into a more complex structure, balancing round and square shapes.
- Above the anda was the harmika, a balcony-like structure that represented the abode of the gods.

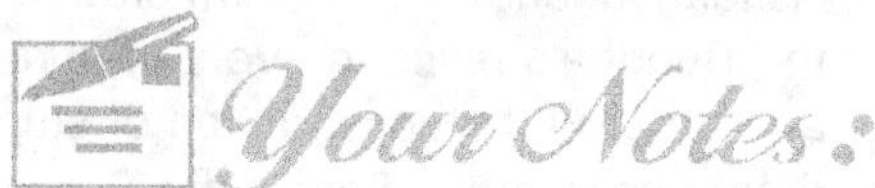 *Your Notes:* ....

CHAPTER 5

THEME FIVE

Through the Eyes of Travellers

Perceptions of Society (c. tenth to seventeenth centuries)

1. Through the Eyes of Travellers

- The chapters talk about the different accounts given by different travellers who came to India from different parts of the world in the medieval period. The accounts that survive are often varied in terms of their subject matter. Some deal with affairs of the court, while others are mainly focused on religious issues, or architectural features and monuments.

- The focusses on the accounts of three men: Al-Biruni who came from Uzbekistan (eleventh century), Ibn Battuta who came from Morocco, in northwestern Africa (fourteenth century) and the Frenchman Franc'ois Bernier (seventeenth century).

1.1 Al-Biruni and the Kitab-ul-Hind

- Al-Biruni was born in 973, in Khwarizm in present-day Uzbekistan.

- In 1017, when Sultan Mahmud invaded Khwarizm, he took several scholars and poets back to his capital, Ghazni; Al-Biruni was one of them.

- He gradually developed a liking for the city, where he spent the rest of his life until his death at the age of 70.

- Al-Biruni spent years in the company of Brahmana priests and scholars, learning Sanskrit, and studying religious and philosophical texts

1.2 The *Kitab-ul-Hind*

- Al-Biruni's *Kitab-ul-Hind* was written in Arabic

- It is a voluminous text, divided into 80 chapters on subjects such as religion and philosophy, festivals, etc.

- Generally (though not always), Al-Biruni adopted a distinctive structure in each chapter, beginning with a question, following this up with a description based on Sanskritic traditions, and concluding with a comparison with other cultures.

2. Ibn Battuta's Rihla

2.1 An early globe-trotter

- Ibn Battuta's book of travels, called *Rihla,* written in Arabic, provides extremely rich and interesting details about the social and cultural life in the subcontinent in the fourteenth century.

- This Moroccan traveller was born in Tangier into one of the most respectable and educated families known for their expertise in Islamic religious law or *shari'a.*

- Travelling overland through Central Asia, Ibn Battuta reached Sind in 1333.

- To meet Muhammad bin Tughlaq, he set off for Delhi, passing through Multan and Uch. The Sultan was impressed by his scholarship, and appointed him the *qazi* or judge of Delhi.

- He was ordered in 1342 to proceed to China as the Sultan's envoy to the Mongol ruler.

- He travelled extensively in China, going as far as Beijing, but did not stay for long, deciding to return home in 1347. His account is often compared with that of Marco Polo, who visited China

- Ibn Battuta was attacked by bands of robbers several times. In fact he preferred travelling in a caravan along with companions.

3. Franc'ois Bernier A Doctor with a Difference

- Among the best known of the Portuguese writers is Duarte Barbosa, who wrote a detailed account of trade and society in south India.

- French jeweller Jean-Baptiste Tavernier travelled to India at least six times.

- Some of these travellers, like the Italian doctor Manucci, never returned to Europe, and settled down in India.

- He was closely associated with the Mughal court, as a physician to Prince Dara Shukoh, the eldest son of Emperor Shah Jahan.

3.1 Comparing "East" and "West"

- Bernier travelled to several parts of the country, and wrote accounts of what he saw, frequently comparing what he saw in India with the situation in Europe.

- He dedicated his major writing to Louis XIV, the king of France, and many of his other works were written in the form of letters to influential officials and ministers

- Bernier's works were published in France in 1670-71 and translated into many other languages.

- Unlike the accounts in Arabic and Persian, which circulated as manuscripts, Bernier's work was reprinted many times.

4. Making Sense of an Alien World Al-Biruni and the Sanskritic Tradition

4.1 Overcoming barriers to understanding

Each traveller adopted distinct strategies to understand what they observed.

Al-Biruni, for instance, discussed several "barriers"

- The first was language. Sanskrit was so different from Arabic and Persian that ideas and concepts could not be easily translated from one language into another.

- The second barrier he identified was the difference in religious beliefs and practices.

- The self-absorption and consequent insularity of the local population according to him, constituted the third barrier.

- Al-Biruni depended almost exclusively on the works of Brahmanas, often citing passages from the Vedas, the Puranas, the *Bhagavad Gita*, the works of Patanjali, the *Manusmriti*, etc.,

4.2 Al-Biruni's description of the caste system

- Al-Biruni attempted to suggest that social divisions were not unique to India.

- He noted that in ancient Persia, four social categories were recognised: those of knights and princes; monks, fire-priests and lawyers; physicians, astronomers and other scientists; and finally, peasants and artisans.

- At the same time he pointed out that within Islam all men were considered equal, differing only in their observance of piety.

- Al-Biruni disapproved of the notion of pollution. He remarked that everything which falls into a state of impurity strives and succeeds in regaining its original condition of purity.

- The conception of social pollution, intrinsic to the caste system, was according to him, contrary to the laws of nature.

- The categories defined as *antyaja* (literally, born outside the system) were often expected to provide inexpensive labour to both peasants and zamindars.

5. Ibn Battuta and the Excitement of the Unfamiliar

5.1 The coconut and the *paan*

His description of the coconut and the pan shows Ibn Battuta's strategies of representation. These are the two kinds of plant produce that were completely unfamiliar to his audience.

5.2 Ibn Battuta and Indian cities

- Ibn Battuta found cities in the subcontinent full of exciting opportunities and which were densely populated and prosperous.

- He described Delhi as a vast city, with a great population, the largest in India. Daulatabad (in Maharashtra) was no less.

- Most bazaars had a mosque and a temple, and in some of them at least, spaces were marked for public performances by dancers, musicians and singers.

- Historians have used his account to suggest that towns derived a significant portion of their wealth through the appropriation of surplus from villages.

- He also noted that the subcontinent was well integrated with inter-Asian networks of trade. Indian textiles, particularly cotton cloth, fine muslins, silks, brocade and satin, were in great demand. Ibn Battuta informs us that certain varieties of fine muslin were so expensive that they could be worn only by the nobles and the very rich

5.3 A unique system of communication

- Almost all trade routes were well supplied with inns and guest houses.

- The postal system used to send information and remit credit across long distances, and also to dispatch goods at short notice.

6. Bernier and the "Degenerate" East

- Franc'ois Bernier was far more occupied with comparison.

- Bernier's *Travels in the Mughal Empire* is marked by detailed observations, critical insights and reflection.

- His representation of India works on the model of binary opposition, where India is presented as the inverse of Europe.

6.1 The question of landownership

- He thought that in the Mughal Empire the emperor owned all the land and distributed it among his nobles, and that this had disastrous consequences for the economy and society.

- This perceptionis found in most travellers' accounts of the sixteenth and seventeenth centuries.

- Owing to crown ownership of land, argued Bernier, landholders could not pass on their land to their children. So they were averse to any long-term investment.

- It had led to the uniform ruination of agriculture, excessive oppression of the peasantry

- Bernier described Indian society as consisting of undifferentiated masses of impoverished people,

- Between the poorest of the poor and the richest of the rich, there was no Middle class.

Mughal's Account:

- For instance, Abu'l Fazl, the sixteenth-century official chronicler of Akbar's reign, describes the land revenue as "remunerations of sovereignty", a claim made by the ruler on his subjects for the protection he provided rather than as rent on land.

Ideological application of Bernier's Narrative:

- Bernier's descriptions influenced Western theorists from the eighteenth century onwards.

- The French philosopher Montesquieu, for instance, used this account to develop the idea of oriental despotism, according to which rulers in Asia (the Orient or the East) enjoyed absolute authority over their subjects.

- This idea was further developed as the concept of the Asiatic mode of production by Karl Marx in the nineteenth century. It was regarded a stagnant system.

Actual situation

- At one end of the spectrum were the big zamindars, who enjoyed superior rights in land and, at the other, the "untouchable" landless

- In between was the big peasant, who used hired labour and engaged in commodity production, and the smaller peasant who could barely produce for his subsistence.

- Bernier drew oversimplified picture of landownership.

- There were all kinds of towns: manufacturing towns, trading towns, port-towns, sacred centres, not just camp towns

6.2 A more complex social reality

- **Bernier** felt that artisans had no incentive to improve the quality of their manufactures, since profits were appropriated by the state.

- He conceded that vast quantities of the world's precious metals flowed into India, as manufactures were exported in exchange for gold and silver. He also noticed the existence of a prosperous merchant community, engaged in long-distance exchange.

- Merchants often had strong community or kin ties, and were organised into their own caste-cum-occupational bodies. In western India these groups were called *mahajans,* and their chief, the *sheth.*

- *The mahajans* were collectively represented by the chief of the merchant community who was called the *nagarsheth.*

- Other urban groups included professional classes such as physicians (*hakim* or *vaid*), teachers (*pundit* or *mulla*), lawyers (*wakil*), painters, architects, musicians, calligraphers, etc.

7. Women - Slaves, Sati and Labourers

- When Ibn Battuta reached Sind he purchased "horses, camels and slaves" as gifts for Sultan Muhammad bin Tughlaq.

- Some female slaves in the service of the Sultan were experts in music and dance, and Ibn Battuta enjoyed their performance.

- Female slaves were also employed by the Sultan to keep a watch on his nobles.

- The price of slaves, particularly female slaves required for domestic labour, was very low

- Women's lives revolved around much else besides the practice of sati. Their labour was crucial in both agricultural and non-agricultural production.

- Women from merchant families participated in commercial activities, sometimes even taking mercantile disputes to the court of law.

Bernier on Sati

- Not surprisingly, Bernier chose the practice of sati for detailed description.

- He noted that while some women seemed to embrace death cheerfully, others were forced to die.

Exercise

Level – 1

1. Al-Biruni generally adopted a distinctive structure in each chapter where the description was based on which of the following traditions?

(a) Sanskritic   (b) Persian

(c) Arabic   (d) None of the Above

2. The term "Hindu" was derived from an Old Persian word that referred to the region which lied to the east of which of the following rivers ?

(a) Sindhu   (b) Sone

(c) Ganges   (d) Saraswati

3. Find the false statements:

(a) Al-Biruni and Ibn Batuta were written in Arabic

(b) Al-Biruni had written Kitab-ul-Hind

(c) Rihla was written by Ibn Batuta

(d) Al-Biruni Kitab-ul-Hind and Rihla were biographies

4. Accounts of which of the following two travellers are compared with respect to the information related to China?

(a) Ibn Batuta and Marco Polo

(b) Marco Polo and Bernier

(c) Duarte Barbosa and Fa Hien

(d) Bernier and Jean-Baptiste Tavernier

5. Franc'ois Bernier, a Frenchman, was associated with whom among the following during his visit to India?

1. Dara Shukoh   2. Danishmand Khan

3. Humanyun

Select the correct answer using the codes given below:

(a) 1 and 2 only   (b) 2 and 3 only

(c) 1 only   (d) 3 only

6. Bernier's account of travels was different from the other accounts in Arabic and Persian in which of the following manner?

(a) Covering the social condition

(b) Section on trade and commerce

(c) Getting reprinted many times

(d) None of the above

7. Which of the following statements is correct with respect to Al Biruni's perception of the social divisions in India?

1. Al-Biruni disapproved of the notion of pollution.

2. Al-Biruni attempted to suggest that social divisions were unique to India.

Select the correct statement using the code given below:

(a) 1 only   (b) 2 only

(c) Both 1 and 2   (d) Neither 1 nor 2

8. Francois Bernier noticed that goods manufactured in India were exported to the world in exchange of which of the following commodities?

(a) Horses   (b) Slaves

(c) Gold and silver   (d) wheat

9. The term 'antyaja' referred to which of the following?

(a) A form of occupation

(b) a form of social division

(c) A form of agricultural practice

(d) A form of festival

10. The description of coconut and the pan was an unfamiliar description by which of the following foreign travellers?

(a) Francois Bernier   (b) Jesuit Roberto Nobili

(c) Duarte Barbosa   (d) Ibn Batuta

Level – 2

11. He was a traveler who came to India during reign of Muhammad-bin-Tughlaq. He was born in Tangier into one of the most respectable and educated families known for their expertise in Islamic religious law or shari'a. The above description is about which of the following travelers?

(a) Megasthenes   (b) Ibn Batuta

(c) Thomas Roe   (d) Nicolo Conti

12. Which of the following places was/were visited by Ibn Batuta?

1. Malabar   2. Maldives

3. Sri Lanka   4. Assam

5. China

Select the correct answer using the codes given below:

(a) 1, 2 and 4 only   (b) 2, 3, 4 and 5 only

(c) 1, 2 and 5 only   (d) 1, 2, 3, 4 and 5

13. Consider the following statements:

1. Italian doctor Manucci visited India 6 times before going back to Europe.

2. French traveller Jean-Baptiste Tavernier came to India once and never returned back.

Which of the statements given above is/are correct?

(a) 1 only   (b) 2 only

(c) Both 1 and 2   (d) Neither 1 nor 2

14. Which of the following statements is/are correct with respect to the work of Al-Biruni?

1. Unlike the other travellers, Al-Biruni did not find language to be the barrier.

2. Al-Biruni depended almost exclusively on the works of Brahmanas.

Select the correct answer using the codes given below:

(a) 1 only   (b) 2 only

(c) Both 1 and 2   (d) Neither 1 nor 2

15. Consider the following statements:

1. Delhi was presented as the second largest city of India after Daulatabad in the deep south.

2. Delhi was know for its great population

Which of the statements given above is/are correct?

(a) 1 only   (b) 2 only

(c) Both 1 and 2   (d) Neither 1 nor 2

16. The strong community or kin ties among the merchants, called mahajans, was especially present in which of the following regions of the Indian subcontinent?

(a) Western   (b) Southern

(c) North east   (d) Northern

17. Which of the following textile materials were exported from India to the world and were are in great demand, as per the accounts of Ibn Batuta?

1. cotton cloth

2. brocade

3. Satin

4. muslin

5. silk

Select the correct statements using the codes given below:

(a) 1, 2 and 4 only   (b) 2, 3, 4 and 5 only

(c) 1, 2 and 5 only   (d) 1, 2, 3, 4 and 5

18. The postal system, as described by Ibn Batuta, but used for which of the following purposes?

1. Send information

2. Remit credit

3. dispatch goods

Select the correct statement using the code given below:

(a) 1 only   (b) 1 and 3 only

(c) 1, 2 and 3 only   (d) 2 only

19. Find the incorrect statement

(a) Jesuit Roberto Nobili had translated many Indian texts into Portuguese languages

(b) Duarte Barbosa wrote a detailed account of trade and society in North India.

(c) Both Duarte Barbosa and Jesuit Roberto were Portuguese writers

(d) Portuguese writers wrote detailed accounts regarding Indian social customs and religious practices

20. The Travels in the Mughal Empire was written by

(a) François Bernier   (b) Hien Tsang

(c) Nicolo Diconti   (d) Manucci

21. Which of the following is/are among the common observations in travellers account India?

1. In the Mughal Empire the emperor owned all the land and distributed it among his nobles.

2. Owing to crown ownership of property, there were disastrous consequences.

Select the correct answer using the codes given below:

(a) 1 only   (b) 2 only

(c) Both 1 and 2   (d) Neither 1 no 2

22. Consider the following statements:

1. Bernier observed that landholders in India could not pass on their land to their children.

2. Bernier's observation of the state as the sole owner of the land was also validated by the Mughal official document.

Which of the statements given above is/are correct?

(a) 1 only   (b) 2 only

(c) Both 1 and 2   (d) Neither 1 nor 2

23. Which of the following travellers outrightly viewed against the existence of the 'middle class' in India?

(a) Ibn Batuta   (b) Megasthenes

(c) Francois Bernier   (d) None of the above

24. Abu'l Fazl was the official chronicler of which of the following Mughal emperor?

(a) Akbar   (b) Aurangzeb

(c) Humayun   (d) Jahangir

25. The concept of the Asiatic mode of production was developed by who among the following thinkers?

(a) Emile Durkheim   (b) GH Mead

(c) Karl Marx   (d) Max Weber

Answers

Level-1

| 1. (a) | 2. (a) | 3. (d) | 4. (a) | 5. (a) | 6. (c) | 7. (a) | 8. (c) | 9. (b) | 10. (d) |

Level-2

| 11. (b) | 12. (d) | 13. (d) | 14. (b) | 15. (b) | 16. (a) | 17. (d) | 18. (c) | 19. (b) | 20. (a) |
| 21. (c) | 22. (a) | 23. (c) | 24. (a) | 25. (c) |

Explanations

Level – 1

1. a Generally (though not always), Al-Biruni adopted a distinctive structure in each chapter, beginning with a question, following this up with a description based on **Sanskritic traditions,** and concluding with a comparison with other cultures.

2. a The term "Hindu" was derived from an Old Persian word, used c. sixth-fifth centuries BCE, to refer to the region east of the river Sindhu (Indus). The Arabs continued the Persian usage and called this region "al-Hind" and its people "Hindi"

3. d Both the books Al-Biruni and Ibn Batuta were written in Arabic. Al-Biruni had written Kitab-ul-Hind while Rihla was written by Ibn Batuta.

These were the travelogue that gave an account of their travels to India

4. a Ibn Batuta travelled extensively in China, going as far as Beijing, but did not stay for long, deciding to return home in 1347. His account is often compared with that of Marco Polo, who visited China

5. a Franc'ois Bernier, a Frenchman, was a doctor, political philosopher and historian. He was closely associated with the Mughal court, as a physician to Prince Dara Shukoh, the eldest son of Emperor Shah Jahan, and later as an intellectual and scientist, with **Danishmand Khan, an Armenian noble at the Mughal court.**

6. c Unlike the accounts in Arabic and Persian, which circulated as manuscripts, Bernier's work was reprinted many times.

7. a Only the first statement is correct

Al-Biruni disapproved of the notion of pollution. He remarked that everything which falls into a state of impurity strives and succeeds in regaining its original condition of purity.

Al-Biruni attempted to suggest that social divisions were not unique to India.

8. c Francois Bernier conceded that vast quantities of the world's precious metals flowed into India, as manufactures were exported in exchange for gold and silver. He also noticed the existence of a prosperous merchant community, engaged in long-distance exchange.

9. b The categories defined as *antyaja* (literally, born outside the system) were often expected to provide inexpensive labour to both peasants and zamindars

10. d The description of the coconut and the pan shows Ibn Battuta's strategies of representation. These are the two kinds of plant produce that were completely unfamiliar to his audience.

Level – 2

11. b The above description is about Ibn Batuta. He was a Moroccan traveller who was born in Tangier into one of the most respectable and educated families known for their expertise in Islamic religious law or *shari'a.*

12. d Ibn Battuta proceeded to the Malabar coast through central India. From Malabar he went to the Maldives, where he stayed for eighteen months as the *qazi,* but eventually decided to proceed to Sri Lanka. He then went back once more to the Malabar coast and the Maldives, and before resuming his mission to China, visited Bengal and Assam as well. He took a ship to Sumatra, a

13. d Both the statements are incorrect.

- Some of these travellers, like the Italian doctor Manucci, never returned to Europe, and settled down in India.

- French jeweller Jean-Baptiste Tavernier travelled to India at least six times.

14. b Only the second statement is correct

Al-Biruni, for instance, d**iscussed several "barriers". The first was language.**Sanskrit was so different from Arabic and Persian that ideas and concepts could not be easily translated from one language into another.

Al-Biruni depended almost **exclusively on the works of Brahmanas**, often citing passages from the Vedas, the Puranas, the *Bhagavad Gita*, the works of Patanjali, the *Manusmriti*, etc.,

15. b Ibn Batuta described **Delhi** as a vast city, with a great population, the largest in India. Daulatabad (in Maharashtra) was no less

16. a Merchants often had strong community or kin ties, and were organised into their own caste-cum-occupational bodies. In western India these groups were called *mahajans,* and their chief, the *sheth.*

17. d Ibn Batuta noted that the subcontinent was well integrated with inter-Asian networks of trade and commerce, with Indian manufactures being in great demand in both West Asia and Southeast Asia, fetching huge profits for artisans and merchants. **Indian textiles, particularly cotton cloth, fine muslins, silks, brocade and satin, were in great demand. Ibn Battuta informs us that certain varieties of fine muslin were so expensive that they** could be worn only by the nobles and the very rich

18. c The postal system, as described by Ibn Batuta, was used to send information and remit credit across long distances, and also to dispatch goods.

19. b Once the Portuguese arrived in India in about 1500, a number of them wrote detailed accounts regarding Indian social customs and religious practices.

A few of them, such as the Jesuit Roberto Nobili, even translated Indian texts into European languages.

Among the best known Portuguese writers is Duarte Barbosa, who wrote a detailed account of trade and society in south India.

20. a Bernier's **Travels in the Mughal Empire is** marked by detailed observations, critical insights and reflection.

21. c Both the statements are correct.

Most travellers thought that in the Mughal Empire the emperor **owned all the land and distributed it** among his nobles and that this had **disastrous consequences for the ec**onomy and society.

This perception was not unique to Bernier, but is found in most travellers' accounts of the sixteenth and seventeenth centuries.

22. a Only the first statement is correct.

Owing to crown ownership of land, argued Ber**nier, landholders could not pass on** their land to their children.

Curiously, none of the Mughal official documents suggests that the state was the sole owner of the land.

23. c Bernier confidently asserted: "There is no middle state in India."

24. a Abu'l Fazl, the sixteenth-century official chronicler of Akbar's reign, describes the land revenue as "remunerations of sovereignty", a claim made by the ruler on his subjects for the protection he provided rather than as rent on land

25. c The idea of oriental despotism was further developed as the concept of the Asiatic mode of production by Karl Marx in the nineteenth century.

CHAPTER 6

THEME SIX

Bhakti-Sufi Traditions

Changes in Religious Beliefs and Devotional Texts (c. eighth to eighteenth century)

1. A Mosaic of Religious Beliefs and Practices

- The most striking feature of this phase - increasing visibility of a wide range of gods (Vishnu, Shiva) and goddesses in sculpture as well as in texts.
- Each of whom was visualised in a variety of forms.

The integration of cults

First processes

- Disseminating Brahmanical ideas.
- Composition, compilation and preservation of Puranic texts in simple Sanskrit verse
- This makes it accessible to women and Shudras, who were generally excluded from Vedic learning.

Second process

- Brahmanas accepting and reworking the beliefs and practices of other social categories.
- Example - Puri, Orissa, where the principal deity was identified, by the twelfth century, as Jagannatha (literally, the lord of the world), a form of Vishnu.

Goddess cults

- Worship of the goddess was evidently widespread and incorporated within the Puranic framework by providing them with an identity as a wife of the principal male deities (eg. Lakshmi, the wife of Vishnu and Parvati, the wife of Shiva.)

Difference and conflict

Tantric

- Often associated with the goddess were forms of worship that were classified as Tantric.
- Tantric practices were widespread in several parts of the subcontinent
- They were open to women and men
- Practitioners often ignored differences of caste and class within the ritual context.

- Many of these ideas influenced Shaivism as well as Buddhism, especially in the eastern, northern and southern parts of the subcontinent.

Discrepancies

- The principal deities of the Vedic pantheon Agni, Indra and Soma, become marginal figures, rarely visible in textual or visual representations.
- And while we can catch a glimpse of Vishnu, Shiva and the goddess in Vedic mantras, these have little in common with the elaborate Puranic mythologies.

Conflicts

- Those who valued the Vedic tradition often condemned practices that went beyond the closely regulated contact with the divine through the performance of sacrifices
- On the other hand those engaged in Tantric practices frequently ignored the authority of the Vedas.
- Devotional worship had a long history of almost a thousand years before the period we are considering.
- The singing and chanting of devotional compositions was often a part of such modes of worship. This was particularly true of the Vaishnava and Shaiva sects.

2. Poems of Prayer Early Traditions of Bhakti

- Poet-saints emerged as leaders around whom there developed a community of devotees. Brahmanas remained important intermediaries between gods and devotees in several forms of bhakti
- These traditions also accommodated and acknowledged women and the "lower castes"
- Earlier these categories were considered ineligible for liberation within the orthodox Brahmanical framework.

Bhakti traditions classified into two broad categories:

- *Saguna* (with attributes)- worship of specific deities such as Shiva, Vishnu and his avatars (incarnations) and forms of the goddess or Devi

- *Nirguna* (without attributes) - worship of an abstract form of god.

The Alvars and Nayanars of Tamil Nadu

Earliest bhakti movements (*c.* sixth century)

- led by the Alvars (literally, those who are "immersed" in devotion to Vishnu) and Nayanars (literally, leaders who were devotees of Shiva).
- They travelled from place to place singing hymns in Tamil in praise of their gods.
- Later the places, were developed as centres of pilgrimage.

Attitudes towards caste

- The Alvars and Nayanars initiated a movement of protest against the caste system and the dominance of Brahmanas
- Bhaktas hailed from diverse social backgrounds ranging from Brahmanas to artisans and cultivators and even from castes considered "untouchable".

Women devotees

- Perhaps one of the most striking features of these traditions was the presence of women.
- Example – Andal (a woman Alvar) - beloved of Vishnu and Karaikkal Ammaiyar, a devotee of Shiva
- These women renounced their social obligations, but did not join an alternative order or become nuns.

Relations with the state

- One of the major themes in Tamil bhakti hymns is the poets' opposition to Buddhism and Jainism.
- This is particularly marked in the compositions of the Nayanars.
- It was due to competition between members of other religious traditions for royal patronage. The powerful Chola rulers (ninth to thirteenth centuries) supported Brahmanical and bhakti traditions, making land grants and constructing temples for Vishnu and Shiva.
- Shiva temples at - Chidambaram, Thanjavur and Gangaikondacholapuram, were constructed under the patronage of Chola rulers.
- Some of the most spectacular representations of Shiva in bronze sculpture were produced. Clearly, the visions of the Nayanars inspired artists.
- Both Nayanars and Alvars were revered by the Vellala peasants, so the rulers tried to win their support
- The rulers introduced the singing of Tamil Shaiva hymns in the temples under royal patronage, taking the initiative to collect and organise them into a text (*Tevaram*).
- Around 945, the Chola ruler Parantaka I had consecrated metal images of Appar, Sambandar and Sundarar in a Shiva temple.

3. The Virashaiva Tradition in Karnataka

- The twelfth century witnessed the emergence of a new movement in Karnataka
- It was led by a Brahmana named Basavanna (1106-68)
- He was a minister in the court of a Kalachuri ruler.
- His followers were known as **Virashaivas** (heroes of Shiva) or Lingayats (wearers of the *linga*).
- Lingayats continue to be an important community in the region to date.
- They worship Shiva in his manifestation as a *linga*
- Men usually wear a small *linga* in a silver case on a loop strung over the left shoulder.
- Those who are revered include the *jangama* or wandering monks.
- Lingayats believe that on death the devotee will be united with Shiva and will not return to this world.
- Therefore they do not practise funerary rites such as cremation, prescribed in the Dharmashastras. Instead, they ceremonially bury their dead.
- The Lingayats challenged the idea of caste and the "pollution" attributed to certain groups by Brahmanas.
- They also questioned the theory of rebirth.
- These won them followers amongst those who were marginalised within the Brahmanical social order.
- The Lingayats also encouraged certain practices disapproved in the Dharmashastras, such as post-puberty marriage and the remarriage of widows.
- Our understanding of the Virashaiva tradition is derived from *vachanas* (literally, sayings) composed in Kannada by women and men who joined the movement.

4. Religious Ferment in North India

- Historians have not found evidence of anything resembling the compositions of the Alvars and Nayanars till the fourteenth century.
- In north India this was the period when several Rajput states emerged.
- In most of these states Brahmanas occupied positions of importance, performing a range of secular and ritual functions.
- There seems to have been little or no attempt to challenge their position directly.
- New religious leaders like Naths, Jogis and Siddhas emerged during that period also failed to win the support of the ruling elites.
- A new element in this situation was the coming of the Turks which culminated in the establishment of the Delhi Sultanate (thirteenth century).

- This undermined the power of many of the Rajput states and the Brahmanas who were associated with these kingdoms.
- This was accompanied by marked changes in the realm of culture and religion.
- The coming of the sufis was a significant part of these developments.

5. New Strands in the Fabric Islamic Traditions

- In 711 an Arab general named Muhammad Qasim conquered Sind, which became part of the Caliph's domain.
- Later (*c.* thirteenth century) the Turks and Afghans established the Delhi Sultanate.
- This was followed by the formation of Sultanates in the Deccan and other parts of the subcontinent
- Islam was an acknowledged religion of rulers in several areas.
- This continued with the establishment of the Mughal Empire in the sixteenth century as well as in many of the regional states that emerged in the eighteenth century.
- The category of the *zimmi,* meaning protected (derived from the Arabic word *zimma*, protection) developed for people who followed revealed scriptures, such as the Jews and Christians, and lived under Muslim rulership.
- They paid a tax called *jizya* and gained the right to be protected by Muslims.
- In India this status was extended to Hindus as well.

The popular practice of Islam

- All those who adopted Islam accepted, in principle, the five "pillars" of the faith: that there is one God, Allah, and Prophet Muhammad is his messenger (*shahada*); offering prayers five times a day (*namaz/ salat*); giving alms (*zakat*); fasting during the month of Ramzan (*sawm*); and performing the pilgrimage to Mecca (*hajj*).

Names for communities

- The term *musalman* or Muslim was virtually never used.
- Instead, people were occasionally identified in terms of the region from which they came.
- A more general term for these migrant communities was *mlechchha*, indicating that they did not observe the norms of caste society and spoke languages that were not derived from Sanskrit.

6. The Growth of Sufism

- In the early centuries of Islam a group of religious-minded people called sufis turned to asceticism and mysticism in protest against the growing materialism of the Caliphate as a religious and political institution.

- They were critical of the dogmatic definitions and scholastic methods of interpreting the Qur'an and *sunna* (traditions of the Prophet) adopted by theologians.
- Instead, they laid emphasis on seeking salvation through intense devotion and love for God by following His commands, and by following the example of the Prophet Muhammad whom they regarded as a perfect human being.
- The sufis thus sought an interpretation of the Qur'an on the basis of their personal experience.

Khanqahs and *silsilas*

- By the eleventh century Sufism evolved into a well-developed movement with a body of literature on Quranic studies and sufi practices.
- Institutionally, the sufis began to organise communities around the hospice or *khanqah* (Persian) controlled by a teaching master known as *shaikh* (in Arabic), *pir* or *murshid* (in Persian).
- He enrolled disciples (*murids*) and appointed a successor (*khalifa*).
- Sufi *silsilas* began to crystallise in different parts of the Islamic world around the twelfth century.
- The word *silsila* literally means a chain, signifying a continuous link between master and disciple, stretching as an unbroken spiritual genealogy to the Prophet Muhammad.
- It was through this channel that spiritual power and blessings were transmitted to devotees.
- Special rituals of initiation were developed in which initiates took an oath of allegiance, wore a patched garment, and shaved their hair.
- When the *shaikh* died, his tomb-shrine (*dargah,* a Persian term meaning court) became the centre of devotion for his followers.
- This encouraged the practice of pilgrimage or *ziyarat* to his grave, particularly on his death anniversary or *urs* (or marriage, signifying the union of his soul with God).

Outside the *khanqah*

- Some mystics initiated movements based on a radical interpretation of sufi ideals.
- Many scorned the *khanqah* and took to mendicancy and observed celibacy.
- They ignored rituals and observed extreme forms of asceticism.
- They were known by different names – Qalandars, Madaris, Malangs, Haidaris, etc.
- Because of their deliberate defiance of the *shari'a* they were often referred to as *be-shari'a*, in contrast to the *ba-shari'a* sufis who complied with it.

7. The Chishtis in the Subcontinent

- Of the groups of sufis who migrated to India in the late twelfth century, the Chishtis were the most influential.
- This was because they adapted successfully to the local environment and adopted several features of Indian devotional traditions.

Life in the Chishti *khanqah*

- The *khanqah* was the centre of social life.

Shaikh Nizamuddin's hospice (*c.* fourteenth century)

- On the banks of the river Yamuna in Ghiyaspur, outskirts of Delhi
- It comprised several small rooms and a big hall (*jama'at khana*) where the inmates and visitors lived and prayed.
- There was an open kitchen (*langar*), run on *futuh* (unasked-for charity).
- People from all walks of life – soldiers, slaves, singers, merchants, poets, travellers, rich and poor, Hindu *jogis* (yogi) and *qalandars* – came seeking discipleship, amulets for healing, and the intercession of the Shaikh in various matters.
- Poets such as Amir Hasan Sijzi and Amir Khusrau and the court historian Ziyauddin Barani, all of whom wrote about the Shaikh.

Chishti devotionalism: *ziyarat* and *qawwali*

- Pilgrimage, called *ziyarat,* to tombs of sufi saints is prevalent all over the Muslim world.
- This practice is an occasion for seeking the sufi's spiritual grace (*barakat*).
- Also part of *ziyarat* is the use of music and dance including mystical chants performed by specially trained musicians or *qawwals* to evoke divine ecstasy.
- The sufis remember God either by reciting the *zikr* (the Divine Names) or evoking His Presence through *sama'* (literally, "audition") or performance of mystical music.
- *Sama'* was integral to the Chishtis, and exemplified interaction with indigenous devotional traditions.
- For more than seven centuries people of various creeds, classes and social backgrounds have expressed their devotion at the *dargahs* of the five great Chishti saints
- Amongst these, the most revered shrine is that of Khwaja Muinuddin, popularly known as "Gharib Nawaz" (comforter of the poor).

Khwaja Muinuddin's dargah

- Muhammad bin Tughlaq (ruled, 1324-51) was the first Sultan to visit the shrine

- The earliest construction to house the tomb was funded in the late fifteenth century by Sultan Ghiyasuddin Khalji of Malwa.
- The shrine was located on the trade route linking Delhi and Gujarat, it attracted a lot of travellers.
- Akbar visited the tomb fourteen times, sometimes two or three times a year,

Languages and communication

- It was not just in *sama'* that the Chishtis adopted local languages.
- In Delhi, those associated with the Chishti *silsila* conversed in Hindavi, the language of the people.
- Other sufis such as Baba Farid composed verses in the local language, which were incorporated in the *Guru Granth Sahib*.
- Other example, the *prem-akhyan* (love story) *Padmavat* composed by Malik Muhammad Jayasi revolved around the romance of Padmini and Ratansen, the king of Chittor.
- Such poetic compositions were often recited in hospices, usually during *sama'*.

Short poems in Dakhani

- A different genre of sufi poetry
- It was composed in and around the town of Bijapur, Karnataka.
- These were short poems in Dakhani (a variant of Urdu) attributed to Chishti sufis who lived in this region during the seventeenth and eighteenth centuries.
- These poems were probably sung by women while performing household chores like grinding grain and spinning.

Other compositions

- Other compositions were in the form of *lurinama* or lullabies and *shadinama*. It is likely that the sufis of this region were inspired by the pre-existing bhakti tradition of the Kannada *vachanas* of the Lingayats and the Marathi *abhangs* of the *sants* of Pandharpur.
- It is through this medium that Islam gradually gained a place in the villages of the Deccan.

Sufis and the state

- A major feature of the Chishti tradition was austerity, including maintaining a distance from worldly power.
- This was by no means a situation of absolute isolation from political power.
- The sufis accepted unsolicited grants and donations from the political elites.
- The Sultans in turn set up charitable trusts (*auqaf*) as endowments for hospices and granted tax-free land (*inam*).
- The Chishtis accepted donations in cash and kind

8. New Devotional Paths Dialogue and Dissent in Northern India

- Many poet-saints engaged in explicit and implicit dialogue with these new social situations, ideas and institutions.

Weaving a divine fabric: Kabir

- Fourteenth-fifteenth centuries
- Verses ascribed to Kabir have been compiled in three distinct but overlapping traditions.
- The *Kabir Bijak* is preserved by the Kabirpanth (the path or sect of Kabir) in Varanasi and elsewhere in Uttar Pradesh
- The *Kabir Granthavali* is associated with the Dadupanth in Rajasthan, and many of his compositions are found in the *Adi Granth Sahib*
- All these manuscript compilations were made long after the death of Kabir.
- Kabir's poems have survived in several languages and dialects; and some are composed in the special language of *nirguna* poets, the *sant bhasha*.
- Others, known as *ulatbansi* (upside-down sayings), are written in a form in which everyday meanings are inverted.
- Diverse and sometimes conflicting ideas are expressed in these poems.

Baba Guru Nanak and the Sacred Word

- Baba Guru Nanak (1469-1539)
- He was born in a Hindu merchant family in a village called Nankana Sahib near the river Ravi in the predominantly Muslim Punjab.
- He trained to be an accountant and studied Persian.
- He was married at a young age but he spent most of his time among sufis and bhaktas.
- The message of Baba Guru Nanak is spelt out in his hymns and teachings.
- These suggest that he advocated a form of *nirguna* bhakti.
- He rejected sacrifices, ritual baths, image worship, austerities and the scriptures of both Hindus and Muslims.
- For Baba Guru Nanak, the Absolute or "*rab*" had no gender or form.
- He proposed a simple way to connect to the Divine by remembering and repeating the Divine Name, expressing his ideas through hymns called "*shabad*" in Punjabi, the language of the region.

- Baba Guru Nanak would sing these compositions in various *ragas* while his attendant Mardana played the *rabab.*
- Baba Guru Nanak organised his followers into a community.
- He set up rules for congregational worship (*sangat*) involving collective recitation.
- He appointed one of his disciples, Angad, to succeed him as the preceptor (*guru*), and this practice was followed for nearly 200 years.
- After his death his followers consolidated their own practices and distinguished themselves from both Hindus and Muslims.
- The fifth preceptor, Guru Arjan, compiled Baba Guru Nanak's hymns along with those of his four successors and other religious poets like Baba Farid, Ravidas (also known as Raidas) and Kabir in the *Adi Granth Sahib.*
- These hymns, called "*gurbani*", are composed in various languages.
- In the late seventeenth century the tenth preceptor, Guru Gobind Singh, included the compositions of the ninth guru, Guru Tegh Bahadur, and this scripture was called the *Guru Granth Sahib.*
- Guru Gobind Singh also laid the foundation of the Khalsa Panth (army of the pure) and defined its five symbols: uncut hair, a dagger, a pair of shorts, a comb and a steel bangle. Under him the community got consolidated as a socio-religious and military force.

Mirabai, the devotee princess

- Fifteenth-sixteenth centuries
- Woman poet within the bhakti tradition.
- She was a Rajput princess from Merta in Marwar who was married against her wishes to a prince of the Sisodia clan of Mewar, Rajasthan.
- She defied her husband and did not submit to the traditional role of wife and mother, instead recognising Krishna, the *avatar* of Vishnu, as her lover.
- Her in-laws tried to poison her, but she escaped from the palace to live as a wandering saint composing songs that are characterised by intense expressions of emotion.
- Mirabai did not attract a sect or group of followers, she has been recognised as a source of inspiration for centuries.

Exercise

Level – 1

1. Who among the following laid the foundation of the Khalsa Panth?

(a) Guru Gobind Singh (b) Guru Nanak

(c) Guru Ravidas (d) Guru Tegh Bahadur

2. Compilations of Kabir's poem are found in which of the following books?

(a) Gurbani (b) Adi Granth Sahib

(c) Sangat (d) None of the above

3. A different genre of sufi short poems was composed in and around the town of Bijapur, Karnataka in Dakhani

Dakhani was a variant of which of the following languages

(a) Arabia (b) Urdu

(c) Iurinama (d) Sama

4. Padmavat was composed by

(a) Malik Muhammad (b) Ratansen

(c) Amir Khusrau (d) Ziyauddin Barani

5. Which of the following Gurus compiled Baba Guru Nanak's hymns?

(a) Guru Arjan (b) Guru Gobind Singh

(c) Guru Ravidas (d) Guru Tegh Bahadur

6. Kabir Bijak, *one of the* verses ascribed to Kabir, is preserved in which of the following states?

(a) Uttar Pradesh (b) Gujrat

(c) Rajasthan (d) Uttrakhand

7. Who among the following authors/historians wrote about Shaikh Nizamuddin's hospice

(a) Amir Hasan Sijzi (b) Amir Khusrau

(c) Ziyauddin Barani (d) All of the above

8. The category of the *zimmi,* developed for people who followed revealed scriptures, such as the Jews and Christians, and lived under Muslim rulership.

Zimmi signifies

(a) protected (b) Taxed

(c) devoted (d) administration

9. Which of the following Sufi's composed verses was incorporated in the Guru Granth Sahib.

(a) Baba Farid

(b) Shaikh Nizamuddin

(c) Malik Muhammad Jayasi

(d) Amir Hasan Sijzi

10. The twelfth century witnessed the emergence of Virashaiva Tradition in which of the following states?

(a) Karnataka (b) Andhra Pradesh

(c) Telangana (d) Tamil Nadu

11. Shiva temples at Chidambaram, Thanjavur and Gangaikondacholapuram, were constructed under the patronage of which of the following rulers?

(a) Chola rulers (b) Chera rulers

(c) Vijaynagar rulers (d) Pandya rulers

12. Earliest bhakti movements were led by which of the following devotees?

(a) Alvar (b) Nayanars

(c) *Saguna* (d) Both a and b

Level – 2

13. Find the correct statement about Kabir

(a) Kabir's poems have survived in several languages and dialects

(b) Kabir's manuscript compilations were made long after his death

(c) Diverse and conflicting ideas are expressed in Kabir's poem

(d) All of the above

14. Find the correct statement about Lingayats

(a) They worship Vishnu

(b) The Lingayats supported the idea of caste

(c) They questioned the theory of rebirth

(d) They practise funerary rites such as cremation

15. Find the false statement about Mirabai

(a) Mirabai did not attract a sect or group of followers

(b) She recognising Rama, the *avatar* of Vishnu, as her lover.

(c) She was a woman poet within the bhakti tradition

(d) She was a Rajput princess

16. Guru Gobind Singh laid the foundation of the Khalsa Panth and defined its five symbols

Which of the following is not among those five symbols:

(a) uncut hair

(b) a dagger

(c) a scarf

(d) a comb

(e) a steel bangle

17. Find the true statement about Khwaja Muinuddin's dargah
    (a) Muhammad bin Tughlaq was the first Sultan to visit the shrine
    (b) The construction to house the tomb was funded by Muhammad bin Tughlaq
    (c) Akbar never visited the dargah
    (d) It was destroyed in the late fifteenth century by Sultan Ghiyasuddin Khalji of Malwa.

18. Find the true statement about Chishtis
    (a) Chishti's followed absolute isolation from political power
    (b) They rejected unsolicited grants and donations from the political elites.
    (c) The Chishtis accepted donations in cash and kind
    (d) Both (a) and (b)

19. Bhakti traditions were classified into which of the following broad category ?
    (a) Saguna and Nirguna (b) Alvars and Nayanars
    (c) Both (a) and (b)   (d) None of the above

20. Sufi compositions in the form of *lurinama* or lullabies and *shadinama* were inspired by which of the following traditions?
    (a) Kannada vachanas (b) Hindavi
    (c) Marathi abhangs   (d) Both (a) and (c)

21. Which of the following Gurus set up rules for congregational worship (*sangat*) involving collective recitation.
    (a) Baba Guru Nanak   (b) Angad
    (c) Nankana Sahib   (d) None of the above

22. The words '*zikr*' and '*Sama*' are associated with which of the following traditions?
    (a) Sufis   (b) Chishti
    (c) Tantric   (d) Lingayat

23. *Sama*' was integral to _
    (a) the five great Chishti saints
    (b) the Chishtis
    (c) dargahs
    (d) Gharib Nawaz

Answers

Level-1

1. (a)	2. (b)	3. (b)	4. (a)	5. (a)	6. (a)	7. (d)	8. (a)	9. (a)	10. (a)

11. (a)	12. (d)

Level-2

13. (d)	14. (c)	15. (b)	16. (c)	17. (a)	18. (c)	19. (a)	20. (d)	21. (a)	22. (a)

23. (b)

Explanations

Level – 1

1. a
- Guru Gobind Singh also laid the foundation of the Khalsa Panth (army of the pure) and defined its five symbols: uncut hair, a dagger, a pair of shorts, a comb and a steel bangle. Under him the community got consolidated as a socio-religious and military force.

2. b
- Verses ascribed to Kabir have been compiled in three distinct but overlapping traditions.
- The *Kabir Granthavali* is associated with the Dadupanth in Rajasthan, and many of his compositions are found in the *Adi Granth Sahib*

3. b
- A different genre of sufi poetry was composed in and around the town of Bijapur, Karnataka.
- These were short poems in Dakhani (a variant of Urdu) attributed to Chishti sufis who lived in this region during the seventeenth and eighteenth centuries.

4. a
- The *prem-akhyan* (love story) *Padmavat* composed by Malik Muhammad Jayasi revolved around the romance of Padmini and Ratansen, the king of Chittor.

5. a
- Guru Arjan, compiled Baba Guru Nanak's hymns along with those of his four successors and other religious poets like Baba Farid, Ravidas (also known as Raidas) and Kabir in the *Adi Granth Sahib*.

6. a
- The *Kabir Bijak* is preserved by the Kabirpanth (the path or sect of Kabir) in Varanasi and elsewhere in Uttar Pradesh

7. d
- Poets such as Amir Hasan Sijzi and Amir Khusrau and the court historian Ziyauddin Barani, all of whom wrote about the Shaikh.

8. a
- The category of the *zimmi,* meaning protected (derived from the Arabic word *zimma,* protection) developed for people who followed revealed scriptures, such as the Jews and Christians, and lived under Muslim rulership.

9. a
- Other sufis such as Baba Farid composed verses in the local language, which were incorporated in the *Guru Granth Sahib*.

10. a
- The twelfth century witnessed the emergence of a new movement in Karnataka
- It was led by a Brahmana named Basavanna (1106-68)
- He was a minister in the court of a Kalachuri ruler.

11. a
- The powerful Chola rulers (ninth to thirteenth centuries) supported Brahmanical and bhakti traditions, making land grants and constructing temples for Vishnu and Shiva.
- Shiva temples at - Chidambaram, Thanjavur and Gangaikondacholapuram, were constructed under the patronage of Chola rulers.

12. d
- Earliest bhakti movements were led by the Alvars (literally, those who are "immersed" in devotion to Vishnu) and Nayanars (literally, leaders who were devotees of Shiva).
- They travelled from place to place singing hymns in Tamil in praise of their gods.
- Later the places, were developed as centres of pilgrimage.

Level – 2

13. d
- All the manuscript compilations were made long after the death of Kabir.
- Kabir's poems have survived in several languages and dialects; and some are composed in the special language of *nirguna* poets, the *sant bhasha*.
- Diverse and sometimes conflicting ideas are expressed in these poems.

14. c
- They worship Shiva in his manifestation as a *linga*
- They do not practise funerary rites such as cremation, prescribed in the Dharmashastras. Instead, they ceremonially bury their dead.
- The Lingayats challenged the idea of caste and the "pollution" attributed to certain groups by Brahmanas.
- They also questioned the theory of rebirth.

15. b
- She is perhaps the best-known woman poet within the bhakti tradition.
- She was a Rajput princess from Merta in Marwar
- She defied her husband and did not submit to the traditional role of wife and mother, instead recognising Krishna, the *avatar* of Vishnu, as her lover.
- Mirabai did not attract a sect or group of followers, she has been recognised as a source of inspiration for centuries.

16. c • Guru Gobind Singh laid the foundation of the Khalsa Panth (army of the pure) and defined its five symbols: uncut hair, a dagger, a pair of shorts, a comb and a steel bangle. Under him the community got consolidated as a socio-religious and military force.

17. a • Muhammad bin Tughlaq (ruled, 1324-51) was the first Sultan to visit the shrine

• The earliest construction to house the tomb was funded in the late fifteenth century by Sultan Ghiyasuddin Khalji of Malwa.

• The shrine was located on the trade route linking Delhi and Gujarat, it attracted a lot of travellers.

• Akbar visited the tomb fourteen times, sometimes two or three times a year,

18. c • A major feature of the Chishti tradition was austerity, including maintaining a distance from worldly power.

• This was by no means a situation of absolute isolation from political power.

• The sufis accepted unsolicited grants and donations from the political elites.

• The Chishtis accepted donations in cash and kind

19. a Bhakti traditions classified into two broad categories:

• *Saguna* (with attributes)- worship of specific deities such as Shiva, Vishnu and his avatars (incarnations) and forms of the goddess or Devi

• *Nirguna* (without attributes) - worship of an abstract form of god.

20. d • Other compositions were in the form of *lurinama* or lullabies and *shadinama*. It is likely that the sufis of this region were inspired by the pre-existing bhakti tradition of the Kannada *vachanas* of the Lingayats and the Marathi *abhangs* of the *sants* of Pandharpur.

21. a • Baba Guru Nanak organised his followers into a community.

• He set up rules for congregational worship (*sangat*) involving collective recitation.

22. a • The sufis remember God either by reciting the *zikr* (the Divine Names) or evoking His Presence through *sama'* (literally, "audition") or performance of mystical music.

23. b • *Sama'* was integral to the Chishtis, and exemplified interaction with indigenous devotional traditions.

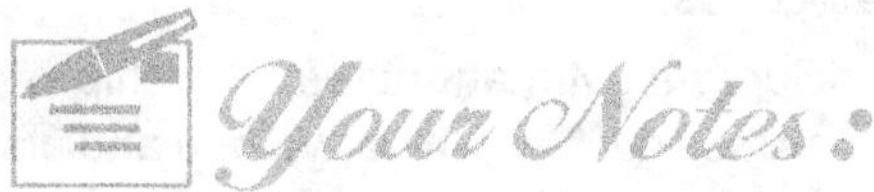

Your Notes : ....

CHAPTER 7

THEME SEVEN

An Imperial Capital Vijayanagara

(c. fourteenth to sixteenth century)

1. Vijayanagara Empire

- The name of both a city and an empire.
- Founded in the fourteenth century.
- It stretched from the river Krishna in the north to the extreme south of the peninsula. (Krishna-Tungabhadra doab)
- In 1565 the city was sacked and subsequently deserted.

The Discovery of Hampi

- Ruins were discovered in 1800
- Hampi, a name derived from that of the local mother goddess, Pampadevi.
- Initial information was based on the memories of priests of the Virupaksha temple and the shrine of Pampadevi.

2. Rayas, Nayakas and Sultans

- Two brothers, Harihara and Bukka, founded the Vijayanagara Empire in 1336.
- Vijaynagar empire northern frontier, rulers –Sultans of the Deccan and the Gajapati rulers of Orissa
- They competed with these rulers for control of the fertile river valleys and the resources generated by lucrative overseas trade.
- At the same time, Interaction between these states led to sharing of ideas, especially in the field of architecture.
- The rulers of Vijayanagara borrowed concepts and building techniques which they then developed further.
- Some of the areas that were incorporated within the empire had witnessed the development of powerful states such as those of the Cholas in Tamil Nadu and the Hoysalas in Karnataka.
- Ruling elites in these areas had extended patronage to elaborate temples such as the Brihadishvara temple at Thanjavur and the Chennakeshava temple at Belur.

- The rulers of Vijayanagara, who called themselves *rayas*, built on these traditions and carried them,

Kings and traders

- The import of horses from Arabia and Central Asia was very important for rival kingdoms.
- This trade was initially controlled by Arab traders.
- Local communities of merchants known as *kudirai chettis* or horse merchants also participated in these exchanges.
- From 1498 Portuguese, who arrived on the west coast of the subcontinent attempted to establish trading and military stations.
- Vijayanagara was also noted for its markets dealing in spices, textiles and precious stones.

The apogee and decline of the empire

- The first dynasty, known as the Sangama dynasty, exercised control till 1485.
- They were supplanted by the Saluvas, military commanders, who remained in power till 1503 when they were replaced by the Tuluvas.
- Krishnadeva Raya belonged to the Tuluva dynasty.
- Krishnadeva Raya's rule was characterised by expansion and consolidation.
- This was the time when the land between the Tungabhadra and Krishna rivers (the Raichur doab) was acquired (1512), the rulers of Orissa were subdued (1514) and severe defeats were inflicted on the Sultan of Bijapur (1520).
- Krishnadeva Raya is credited with building some fine temples and adding impressive *gopurams* to many important south Indian temples.
- He also founded a suburban township near Vijayanagara called Nagalapuram after his mother.
- After the death of Krishnadeva Raya in 1529 the control at the centre had shifted to another ruling lineage, that of the Aravidu

- Aravidu remained in power till the end of the seventeenth century.
- In 1565 Rama Raya, the chief minister of Vijayanagara, led the army into battle at Rakshasi-Tangadi (also known as Talikota), where his forces were routed by the combined armies of Bijapur, Ahmadnagar and Golconda.
- The victorious armies sacked the city of Vijayanagara.
- The city was totally abandoned within a few years.

The *rayas* and the *nayakas*

- Military chiefs exercised power in the empire
- These chiefs were known as *nayakas* and they usually spoke Telugu or Kannada.
- Many *nayakas* submitted to the authority of the kings of Vijayanagara but they often rebelled and had to be subdued by military action.
- The *amara-nayaka* system was a major political innovation of the Vijayanagara Empire.
- It is likely that many features of this system were derived from the *iqta* system of the Delhi Sultanate.
- The *amara-nayakas* were military commanders who were given territories to govern by the *raya*.
- They collected taxes and other dues from peasants, craftspersons and traders in the area.
- They retained part of the revenue for personal use and for maintaining a stipulated contingent of horses and elephants.
- These contingents provided the Vijayanagara kings with an effective fighting force with which they brought the entire southern peninsula under their control.
- The *amara-nayakas* sent tribute to the king annually and personally appeared in the royal court with gifts to express their loyalty.
- Kings occasionally asserted their control over them by transferring them from one place to another.
- However, during the course of the seventeenth century, many of these *nayakas* established independent kingdoms.
- This hastened the collapse of the central imperial structure.

3. Vijayanagara The Capital and its Environs

Water resources

- Natural basin formed by the river Tungabhadra which flows in a north-easterly direction.
- Embankments were built along these streams to create reservoirs of varying sizes.
- As this is one of the most arid zones of the peninsula, elaborate arrangements had to be made to store rainwater and conduct it to the city.

- The most important such tank was built in the early years of the fifteenth century and is now called Kamalapuram tank.
- One of the most prominent waterworks to be seen among the ruins is the Hiriya canal. This canal drew water from a dam across the Tungabhadra and irrigated the cultivated valley that separated the "sacred centre" from the "urban core".
- This was apparently built by kings of the Sangama dynasty.

Fortifications and roads

- Abdur Razzaq, an ambassador sent by the ruler of Persia to Calicut (present-day Kozhikode) in the fifteenth century, was greatly impressed by the fortifications, and mentioned seven lines of forts.
- Most significant about this fortification is that it enclosed agricultural tracts.
- Between the first, second and the third walls there are cultivated fields, gardens and houses.
- From this first circuit until you enter the city there is a great distance, in which are fields in which they sow rice and have many gardens and much water, in which water comes from two lakes.
- Evidence of an agricultural tract between the sacred centre and the urban core.
- This tract was serviced by an elaborate canal system drawing water from the Tungabhadra.
- Instead of making larger granaries the rulers of Vijayanagara adopted a more expensive and elaborate strategy of protecting the agricultural belt itself.

The urban core

- There is relatively little archaeological evidence of the houses of ordinary people.
- These areas may have been occupied by rich traders.
- This was also the Muslim residential quarter.
- Tombs and mosques located here have distinctive functions, yet their architecture resembles that of the *mandapas* found in the temples of Hampi.
- This is how the sixteenth-century Portuguese traveller Barbosa described the houses of ordinary people, which have not survived:
- The entire area was dotted with numerous shrines and small temples,
- Prevalence of a variety of cults, perhaps supported by different communities.

4. The Royal Centre

- The royal centre was located in the south-western part of the settlement.
- It included over 60 temples.

- The patronage of temples and cults was important for rulers
- About thirty building complexes have been identified as palaces.
- These are relatively large structures that do not seem to have been associated with ritual functions.
- One difference between these structures and temples is that the latter were constructed entirely of masonry, while the superstructure of the secular buildings was made of perishable materials.

The mahanavami dibba

- The "king's palace" is the largest of the enclosures but has not yielded definitive evidence of being a royal residence.
- It has two of the most impressive platforms, usually called the "audience hall" and the *"mahanavami dibba"*.
- Located on one of the highest points in the city, the *"mahanavami dibba"* is a massive platform rising from a base of about 11,000 sq. ft to a height of 40 ft.
- There is evidence that it supported a wooden structure. The base of the platform is covered with relief carvings.
- Rituals associated with the structure probably coincided with Mahanavami (literally, the great ninth day) of the ten-day Hindu festival.
- The Vijayanagara kings displayed their prestige, power and suzerainty on this occasion.
- The ceremonies performed on the occasion included worship of the image, worship of the state horse, and the sacrifice of buffaloes and other animals.

Other buildings in the royal centre

- One of the most beautiful buildings in the royal centre is the Lotus Mahal - Not quite sure what the building was used for.
- While most temples were located in the sacred centre, there were several in the royal centre as well (eg. Hazara Rama temple).
- This was probably meant to be used only by the king and his family.

5. The Sacred Centre

Choosing a capital

- Rocky northern end of the city on the banks of the Tungabhadra.
- Temple building in the region had a long history, going back to dynasties such as the Pallavas, Chalukyas, Hoysalas and Cholas.
- Rulers very often encouraged temple building as a means of associating themselves with the divine
- Temples also functioned as centres of learning.

- Temples developed as significant religious, social, cultural and economic centres.
- It is likely that the very choice of the site of Vijayanagara was inspired by the existence of the shrines of Virupaksha and Pampadevi.
- In fact the Vijayanagara kings claimed to rule on behalf of the god Virupaksha.
- All royal orders were signed "Shri Virupaksha", usually in the Kannada script.
- Rulers also indicated their close links with the gods by using the title "Hindu Suratrana".
- This was a Sanskritisation of the Arabic term Sultan, meaning king, so it literally meant Hindu Sultan.

Gopurams and mandapas

- In terms of temple architecture, by this period certain new features were in evidence.
- Structures of immense scale (eg. raya *gopurams* or royal gateways -signalled the presence of the temple from a great distance.
- Other distinctive features include *mandapas* or pavilions and long, pillared corridors that often ran around the shrines within the temple complex.

Virupaksha temple

- The Virupaksha temple
- It was built over centuries.
- The earliest shrine dated to the ninth-tenth centuries, it was substantially enlarged with the establishment of the Vijayanagara Empire.
- The hall in front of the main shrine was built by Krishnadeva Raya to mark his accession.
- He is also credited with the construction of the eastern *gopuram*.
- The halls in the temple were used for a variety of purposes.

Vitthala temple

- Here, the principal deity was Vitthala, a form of Vishnu generally worshipped in Maharashtra. The introduction of the worship of the deity in Karnataka is another indication of the ways in which the rulers of Vijayanagara drew on different traditions to create an imperial culture.
- This temple too has several halls and a unique shrine designed as a chariot
- A characteristic feature of the temple complexes is the chariot streets that extended from the temple *gopuram* in a straight line.
- These streets were paved with stone slabs and lined with pillared pavilions in which merchants set up their shops.

Exercise

Level – 1

1. The most striking feature about the location of Vijayanagara is the natural basin formed by the which of the following rivers?

   (a) Tungabhadra   (b) Bhima

   (c) Krishna   (d) Godavari

2. The surrounding landscape of Vijayanagara was characterised by which of the following physical layouts?

   (a) Granite hills

   (b) Arid zones of the peninsula

   (c) Western ghats

   (d) Eastern ghats

3. The sixteenth-century traveller Barbosa described the houses of ordinary people, which have not survived Traveller Barbosa came from which of the following counties?

   (a) Portuguese   (b) Spain

   (c) Persia   (d) Egypt

4. Gajapati rulers ruled in which of the following regions?

   (a) Orissa

   (b) Gujrat

   (c) Rajasthan

   (d) Madhya Pradesh

5. The rulers of which of the following regions called themselves *rayas*?

   (a) Cholas in Tamil Nadu

   (b) Hoysalas in Karnataka

   (c) Vijayanagara

   (d) None of the above

6. The ruler of which of the following country sent Abdur Razzaq to Calicut in the fifteenth century?

   (a) Persia

   (b) Afghan

   (c) Egypt

   (d) Arab

7. There is archaeological evidence of Muslim residential quarter in which of the areas of the Vijaynagar empire?

   (a) First circuit

   (b) Between the first and second walls

   (c) Urban core

   (d) None of the above

8. In the Vitthala temple of Vijaynagar empire, the principal deity was Vitthala, a form of Vishnu generally worshipped in which of the following states?

   (a) North India   (b) Maharashtra

   (c) Andhra Pradesh   (d) Karnataka

9. Vijayanagara was inspired by the existence of which of the following shrines

   (a) Virupaksha   (b) Pampadevi.

   (c) Vitthala temple   (d) Both (a) and (b)

10. The Vijayanagara Empire was founded in 1336 by who among the following ?

   (a) Harihara   (b) Pampadevi.

   (c) Bukka   (d) Both (a) and (c)

11. Kudirai chettis were

   (a) merchants

   (b) Priests

   (c) *nayakas*

   (d) *Amara*

Level – 2

12. Find the true statement about Hazara Rama temple of Vijaynagar empire

   (a) It was situated in the sacred centre

   (b) It was meant to be used only by the king and his family.

   (c) Sculpted panels on the walls include scenes from the Mahabharata

   (d) None of the above

13. Which of the following waterworks of Vijaynagar empire drew water from a dam across the Tungabhadra and irrigated the cultivated valley that separated the "sacred centre" from the "urban core"?

   (a) Kamalapuram tank

   (b) Hiriya canal.

   (c) Both (a) and (b)

   (d) None of the above

14. Find the true statement about the fortification of Vijayanagara empire

   (a) Between the first, second and the third walls there are cultivated fields

   (b) The fortification encloses agricultural tracts.

   (c) Evidence of an agricultural tract between the sacred centre and the urban core.

   (d) Both (b) and (c)

15. Find the incorrect statement about the agriculture practices of the Vijayanagar empire

(a) Agricultural tract was serviced by an elaborate canal system

(b) The canal system draws water from the Tungabhadra.

(c) They adopted a more expensive and elaborate strategy of protecting the agricultural belt itself

(d) Both (a) and (b)

16. A characteristic feature of the temple complexes is the chariot streets that extended from the temple *gopuram* in a straight line.

The above statement best describes which of the following temples?

(a) Virupaksha temple   (b) Vitthala temple

(c) Jaina temples   (d) None of the above

17. Military chiefs were known as

(a) *nayakas*   (b) *rayas*

(c) *amara-nayakas*   (d) *None of the above*

18. Krishnadeva Raya composed a work on statecraft in Telugu known as

(a) *mahanavami*

(b) Amuktamalyada

(c) Suratrana

(d) None of the above

19. Krishnadeva Raya belonged to which of the following dynasties?

(a) Tuluva dynasty

(b) Rakshasi-Tangadi dynasty

(c) Talikota dynasty

(d) None of the above

20. Find the true statement about Krishnadeva Raya's rule

(a) It was characterised by expansion and consolidation

(b) He is credited with building *gopurams* to many important south Indian temples

(c) He founded a suburban township near Vijayanagara called Nagalapuram

(d) All of the above

21. After the death of Krishnadeva Raya the control at the centre had shifted to which of the following rulers?

(a) Aravidu   (b) Rama Raya

(c) *Amara-nayakas*   (d) *Raya*

22. Raichur doab is between which of the following rivers?

(a) Tungabhadra and Krishna rivers

(b) Krishna rivers and Godavari rivers

(c) Tungabhadra and Cauvery rivers

(d) Krishna and Cauvery rivers

Answers

Level-1

1. (a)   **2.** (a)   **3.** (a)   **4.** (a)   **5.** (c)   **6.** (a)   **7.** (c)   **8.** (b)   **9.** (d)   **10.** (d)

11. (a)

Level-2

12. (b)   **13.** (b)   **14.** (d)   **15.** (c)   **16.** (a)   **17.** (a)   **18.** (b)   **19.** (a)   **20.** (d)   **21.** (a)

22. (a)

Explanations

Level – 1

1. a • Natural basin formed by the river Tungabhadra which flows in a north-easterly direction.

2. a • The city was characterised by stunning granite hills that seem to form a girdle around the city.

3. a • Tombs and mosques located here have distinctive functions, yet their architecture resembles that of the *mandapas* found in the temples of Hampi.

• This is how the sixteenth-century Portuguese traveller Barbosa described the houses of ordinary people, which have not survived:

4. a • On their northern frontier, the Vijayanagara kings competed with contemporary rulers – including the Sultans of the Deccan and the Gajapati rulers of Orissa

5. c • The rulers of Vijayanagara, called themselves *rayas*

6. a • Abdur Razzaq, an ambassador sent by the ruler of Persia to Calicut (present-day Kozhikode) in the fifteenth century, was greatly impressed by the fortifications, and mentioned seven lines of forts.

7. c • In Urban core area there is relatively little archaeological evidence of the houses of ordinary people.

• These areas may have been occupied by rich traders.

• This was also the Muslim residential quarter.

8. b • The Vitthala temple - Here, the principal deity was Vitthala, a form of Vishnu generally worshipped in Maharashtra.

9. d • Vijayanagara was inspired by the existence of the shrines of Virupaksha and Pampadevi. In fact the Vijayanagara kings claimed to rule on behalf of the god Virupaksha.

10. d • According to tradition and epigraphic evidence two brothers, Harihara and Bukka, founded the Vijayanagara Empire in 1336.

11. a • Local communities of merchants known as *kudirai chettis* or horse merchants

Level – 2

12. b • While most temples were located in the sacred centre, there were several in the royal centre as well.

• One of the most spectacular of these is one known as the Hazara Rama temple. This was probably meant to be used only by the king and his family.

• Sculpted panels on the walls survive.

• These include scenes from the *Ramayana* sculpted on the inner walls of the shrine.

13. b • One of the most prominent waterworks to be seen among the ruins is the Hiriya canal. This canal drew water from a dam across the Tungabhadra and irrigated the cultivated valley that separated the "sacred centre" from the "urban core".

14. d • Most significant about this fortification is that it enclosed agricultural tracts.

• Between the first, second and the third walls there are cultivated fields, gardens and houses.

• Evidence of an agricultural tract between the sacred centre and the urban core.

• This tract was serviced by an elaborate canal system drawing water from the Tungabhadra.

15. c • Evidence of an agricultural tract between the sacred centre and the urban core.

• This tract was serviced by an elaborate canal system drawing water from the Tungabhadra.

• The rulers of Vijayanagara adopted a more expensive and elaborate strategy of building large granaries within fortified areas.

16. a

17. a • Military chiefs exercised power in the empire

• These chiefs were known as *nayakas* and they usually spoke Telugu or Kannada.

18. b • Krishnadeva Raya (ruled 1509-29), the most famous ruler of Vijayanagara, composed a work on statecraft in Telugu known as the Amuktamalyada.

19. a • Krishnadeva Raya belonged to the Tuluva dynasty.

20. d • Krishnadeva Raya's rule was characterised by expansion and consolidation.

• Krishnadeva Raya is credited with building some fine temples and adding impressive *gopurams* to many important south Indian temples.

• He also founded a suburban township near Vijayanagara called Nagalapuram after his mother.

21. a • After the death of Krishnadeva Raya in 1529 the control at the centre had shifted to another ruling lineage, that of the Aravidu

• Aravidu remained in power till the end of the seventeenth century.

22. a

CHAPTER 8

Peasants, Zamindars and the State
Agrarian Society and the Mughal Empire
(c. sixteenth-seventeenth centuries)

1. Peasants and Agricultural Production

- The basic unit of agricultural society was the village, inhabited by peasants who performed the manifold seasonal tasks that made up agricultural production throughout the year

Looking for sources

- Major source for the agrarian history - chronicles and documents from the Mughal court

- One of the most important chronicles was the Ain-i Akbari authored by Akbar's court historian Abu'l Fazl.

- It recorded the arrangements made by the state to ensure cultivation, to enable the collection of revenue by the agencies of the state and to regulate the relationship between the state and rural magnates, the zamindars.

- The central purpose of the Ain was to present a vision of Akbar's empire where social harmony was provided by a strong ruling class.

- Other Sources - include detailed revenue records from Gujarat, Maharashtra and Rajasthan dating from the seventeenth and eighteenth centuries.

- The extensive records of the East India Company provide us with useful descriptions of agrarian relations in eastern India.

- All these sources record instances of conflicts between peasants, zamindars and the state.

Peasants and their lands

- The term which Indo-Persian sources of the Mughal period most frequently used to denote a peasant was raiyat or muzarian.

- Sources of the seventeenth century refer to two kinds of peasants – khud-kashta and pahi-kashta.

- khud-kashta - were residents of the village in which they held their lands.

- pahi-kashta - were non-resident cultivators who belonged to some other village, but cultivated lands elsewhere on a contractual basis.

Irrigation and technology

- The abundance of land, available labour and the mobility of peasants were three factors that accounted for the constant expansion of agriculture.

- Basic staples such as rice, wheat or millets were the most frequently cultivated crops.

- Areas which received 40 inches or more of rainfall a year were generally rice-producing zones, followed by wheat and millets, corresponding to a descending scale of precipitation.

Irrigation

- Dependent on Monsoons but there were crops which required additional water.

- Artificial systems of irrigation had to be devised for this.

- Irrigation projects also received state support

An abundance of crops

- Agriculture was organised around two major seasonal cycles, the *kharif* (autumn) and the *rabi* (spring).

- Most regions, except those terrains that were the most arid or inhospitable, produced a minimum of two crops a year, whereas some, where rainfall or irrigation assured a continuous supply of water, even gave three crops.

- This ensured an enormous variety of produce.

- The Mughal provinces of Agra produced 39 varieties of crops and Delhi produced 43 over the two seasons. Bengal produced 50 varieties of rice alone.

jins-i kamil (literally, perfect crops)

- The Mughal state also encouraged peasants to cultivate such crops as they brought in more revenue.
- Crops such as cotton and sugarcane were *jins-i kamil* par excellence.
- Cotton was grown over a great swathe of territory spread over central India and the Deccan plateau, whereas Bengal was famous for its sugar.
- Such cash crops would also include various sorts of oilseeds (for example, mustard) and lentils.
- Maize (*makka*), was introduced into India via Africa and Spain and by the seventeenth century it was being listed as one of the major crops of western India.
- Vegetables like tomatoes, potatoes and chillies were introduced from the New World at this time, as were fruits like the pineapple and the papaya.

2. The Village Community

- Peasants held their lands in individual ownership.
- At the same time they belonged to a collective village community
- There were three constituents of this community – the cultivators, the panchayat, and the village headman (*muqaddam* or *mandal*).

Caste and the rural milieu

Menials

- Among those who tilled the land, there was a sizeable number who worked as menials or agricultural labourers (*majur*).
- Despite the abundance of cultivable land, certain caste groups were assigned menial tasks and thus relegated to poverty.
- Such groups comprised a large section of the village population, had the least resources and were constrained by their position in the caste hierarchy, much like the Dalits of modern India.
- In Muslim communities menials like the *halalkhoran* (scavengers) were housed outside the boundaries of the village
- Similarly the *mallahzadas* (literally, sons of boatmen) in Bihar were comparable to slaves.
- There was a direct correlation between caste, poverty and social status at the lower strata of society.
- Such correlations were not so marked at intermediate levels.
- The Gauravas, who cultivated land around Vrindavan (Uttar Pradesh), sought Rajput status in the seventeenth century.
- Castes such as the Ahirs, Gujars and Malis rose in the hierarchy because of the profitability of cattle rearing and horticulture.

- In the eastern regions, intermediate pastoral and fishing castes like the Sadgops and Kaivartas acquired the status of peasants.

Panchayats and headmen

- The village panchayat was an assembly of elders, usually important people of the village with hereditary rights over their property.
- In mixed-caste villages, the panchayat was usually a heterogeneous body.
- An oligarchy, the panchayat represented various castes and communities in the village, though the village menial-cum-agricultural worker was unlikely to be represented there.
- The decisions made by these panchayats were binding on the members.
- The panchayat was headed by a headman known as *muqaddam* or *mandal.*
- Headmen held office as long as they enjoyed the confidence of the village elders, failing which they could be dismissed by them.
- The chief function of the headman was to supervise the preparation of village accounts, assisted by the accountant or *patwari* of the panchayat.
- The panchayat derived its funds from contributions made by individuals to a common financial pool.
- These funds were used for defraying the costs of entertaining revenue officials who visited the village from time to time.
- One important function of the *panchayat* was to ensure that caste boundaries among the various communities inhabiting the village were upheld.
- In eastern India all marriages were held in the presence of the *mandal.*
- One of the duties of the village headman was to oversee the conduct of the members of the village community "chiefly to prevent any offence against their caste".
- Panchayats also had the authority to levy fines and inflict more serious forms of punishment like expulsion from the community.
- In addition to the village panchayat each caste or jati in the village had its own jati panchayat.
- These panchayats wielded considerable power in rural society.
- In Rajasthan jati panchayats arbitrated civil disputes between members of different castes.
- In most cases, except in matters of criminal justice, the state respected the decisions of jati panchayats.
- Village panchayat was regarded as the court of appeal that would ensure that the state carried out its moral obligations and guaranteed justice.

Village artisans

- There were substantial numbers of artisans, sometimes as high as 25 per cent of the total households in the villages.
- The distinction between artisans and peasants in village society was a fluid one, as many groups performed the tasks of both.
- Cultivators and their families would also participate in craft production – such as dyeing, textile printing, baking and firing of pottery, making and repairing agricultural implements.
- Village artisans – potters, blacksmiths, carpenters, barbers, even goldsmiths – provided specialised services in return for which they were compensated by villagers by a variety of means.
- The most common way of doing so was by giving them a share of the harvest, or an allotment of land, perhaps cultivable wastes, which was likely to be decided by the panchayat.
- In Maharashtra such lands became the artisans' *miras* or *watan* – their hereditary holding.
- Another variant of this was a system where artisans and individual peasant households entered into a mutually negotiated system of remuneration, most of the time goods for services.
- For example, eighteenth-century records tell us of zamindars in Bengal who remunerated blacksmiths, carpenters, even goldsmiths for their work by paying them "a small daily allowance and diet money".
- This later came to be described as the *jajmani* system, though the term was not in vogue in the sixteenth and seventeenth centuries.
- Cash remuneration was not entirely unknown either.

3. Women in Agrarian Society

- Women and men had to work shoulder to shoulder in the fields.
- Men tilled and ploughed, while women sowed, weeded, threshed and winnowed the harvest. With the growth of nucleated villages and expansion in individuated peasant farming, which characterised medieval Indian agriculture, the basis of production was the labour and resources of the entire household.
- Naturally, a gendered segregation between the home (for women) and the world (for men) was not possible in this context.
- Nonetheless biases related to women's biological functions did continue.
- Menstruating women, for instance, were not allowed to touch the plough or the potter's wheel in western India, or enter the groves where betel-leaves (*paan*) were grown in Bengal.

- Artisanal tasks such as spinning yarn, sifting and kneading clay for pottery, and embroidery were among the many aspects of production dependent on female labour.
- Women were considered an important resource in agrarian society also because they were child bearers in a society dependent on labour.
- At the same time, high mortality rates among women – owing to malnutrition, frequent pregnancies, death during childbirth – often meant a shortage of wives.
- This led to the emergence of social customs in peasant and artisan communities that were distinct from those prevalent among elite groups.
- Marriages in many rural communities required the payment of bride-price rather than dowry to the bride's family.
- Remarriage was considered legitimate both among divorced and widowed women.
- The household was headed by a male. Thus women were kept under strict control by the male members of the family and the community.
- They could inflict draconian punishments if they suspected infidelity on the part of women.
- Amongst the landed gentry, women had the right to inherit property.
- Hindu and Muslim women inherited zamindaris which they were free to sell or mortgage.
- Women zamindars were known in eighteenth-century Bengal.

4. Forests and Tribes

Beyond settled villages

- Apart from the intensively cultivated provinces in northern and north-western India, huge swathes of forests – dense forest (*jangal*) or scrubland (*kharbandi*) – existed all over eastern India, central India, northern India (including the Terai on the Indo-Nepal border), Jharkhand, and in peninsular India down the Western Ghats and the Deccan plateau.
- Forest dwellers were termed *jangli* in contemporary texts.
- The term described those whose livelihood came from the gathering of forest produce, hunting and shifting agriculture.
- These activities were largely season specific.
- Eg – Bhils, spring was reserved for collecting forest produce, summer for fishing, the monsoon months for cultivation, and autumn and winter for hunting.
- For the state, the forest was a subversive place – a place of refuge (*mawas*) for troublemakers.

Inroads into forests

- External forces entered the forest in different ways.
- Forest products – like honey, beeswax and gum lac – were in great demand.
- Some, such as gum lac, became major items of overseas export from India in the seventeenth century.
- Elephants were also captured and sold.
- Trade involved an exchange of commodities through barter as well.
- Some tribes, like the Lohanis in the Punjab, were engaged in overland trade, between India and Afghanistan
- Many tribal chiefs had become zamindars, some even became kings. For this they required to build up an army. They recruited people from their lineage groups
- Tribes in the Sind region had armies comprising 6,000 cavalry and 7,000 infantry.
- In Assam, the Ahom kings had their *paiks*, people who were obliged to render military service in exchange for land.
- The capture of wild elephants was declared a royal monopoly by the Ahom kings.
- Though the transition from a tribal to a monarchical system had started much earlier, the process seems to have become fully developed only by the sixteenth century.

5. The Zamindars

- Zamindars - class of people in the countryside that lived off agriculture but did not participate directly in the processes of agricultural production.
- They were landed proprietors who also enjoyed certain social and economic privileges by virtue of their superior status in rural society.
- Caste was one factor that accounted for the elevated status of zamindars
- They performed certain services (*khidmat*) for the state.
- The zamindars held extensive personal lands termed *milkiyat,* meaning property.
- *Milkiyat* lands were cultivated for the private use of zamindars, often with the help of hired or servile labour.
- The zamindars could sell, bequeath or mortgage these lands at will.
- Zamindars also derived their power from the fact that they could often collect revenue on behalf of the state
- Control over military resources was another source of power.

- Most zamindars had fortresses (*qilachas*) as well as an armed contingent comprising units of cavalry, artillery and infantry.
- Abu'l Fazl's account indicates that an "upper-caste", Brahmana-Rajput combine had already established firm control over rural society.
- The dispossession of weaker people by a powerful military chieftain was quite often a way of expanding a zamindari.
- The slow processes of zamindari consolidation involved colonisation of new lands, by transfer of rights, by order of the state and by purchase.
- These were the processes which perhaps permitted people belonging to the relatively "lower" castes to enter the rank of zamindars as zamindaris were bought and sold quite briskly in this period.
- A combination of factors also allowed the consolidation of clan- or lineage-based zamindaris.
- For example, the Rajputs and Jats adopted these strategies to consolidate their control over vast swathes of territory in northern India.
- Likewise, peasant-pastoralists (like the Sadgops) carved out powerful zamindaris in areas of central and south- western Bengal.
- Zamindars spearheaded the colonisation of agricultural land
- They helped in settling cultivators by providing them with the means of cultivation, including cash loans.
- The buying and selling of zamindaris accelerated the process of monetisation in the countryside.
- Zamindars often established markets (*haats*) to which peasants also came to sell their produce.
- Their relationship with the peasantry had an element of reciprocity, paternalism and patronage.

Two aspects reinforce this view.

- First, the bhakti saints, who eloquently condemned caste-based and other forms of oppression did not portray the zamindars as exploiters of the peasantry. Usually it was the revenue official of the state who was the object of their ire.
- Second, in a large number of agrarian uprisings which erupted in north India in the seventeenth century, zamindars often received the support of the peasantry in their struggle against the state.

6. Land Revenue System

- Revenue from the land was the economic mainstay of the Mughal Empire.
- The land revenue arrangements consisted of two stages – first, assessment and then actual collection.

- The *jama* was the amount assessed, as opposed to *hasil*, the amount collected.
- In his list of duties of the *amil-guzar* or revenue collector, Akbar decreed that while he should strive to make cultivators pay in cash, the option of payment in kind was also to be kept open.

7. The Flow of Silver

- The Mughal Empire was among the large territorial empires in Asia that had managed to consolidate power and resources during the sixteenth and seventeenth centuries.
- These empires were the Ming (China), Safavid (Iran) and Ottoman (Turkey).
- The political stability achieved by all these empires helped create vibrant networks of overland trade from China to the Mediterranean Sea.
- Voyages of discovery and the opening up of the New World resulted in a massive expansion of Asia's (particularly India's) trade with Europe.
- Expanding trade brought in huge amounts of silver bullion into Asia to pay for goods procured from India, and a large part of that bullion gravitated towards India.
- This was good for India as it did not have natural resources of silver.
- As a result, the period between the sixteenth and eighteenth centuries was also marked by a remarkable stability in the availability of metal currency, particularly the silver *rupya* in India.
- This facilitated an unprecedented expansion of minting of coins and the circulation of money in the economy as well as the ability of the Mughal state to extract taxes and revenue in cash.

8. The Ain-i Akbari of Abu'l Fazl Allami

- Culmination of a large historical, administrative project of classification undertaken by Abu'l Fazl at the order of Emperor Akbar.
- It was completed in 1598
  - The *Ain* was part of a larger project of history writing commissioned by Akbar.
  - This history, known as the *Akbar Nama,* comprised three books.
  - The first two provided a historical narrative.
  - The *Ain-i Akbari*, the third book, was organised as a compendium of imperial regulations and a gazetteer of the empire.

- The *Ain* gives detailed accounts of the organisation of the court, administration and army, the sources of revenue and the physical layout of the provinces of Akbar's empire and the literary, cultural and religious traditions of the people.
- The *Ain* is made up of five books (*daftars*), of which the first three books describe the administration.
- The first book, called *manzil-abadi*, concerns the imperial household and its maintenance.
- The second book, *sipah-abadi*, covers the military and civil administration and the establishment of servants.
- This book includes notices and short biographical sketches of imperial officials (*mansabdars*), learned men, poets and artists.
- The third book, *mulk-abadi*, is the one which deals with the fiscal side of the empire and provides rich quantitative information on revenue rates, followed by the "Account of the Twelve Provinces".
- This section has detailed statistical information, which includes the geographic, topographic and economic profile of all *subas and* their administrative and fiscal divisions (*sarkars, parganas* and *mahals*), total measured area, and assessed revenue (*jama*).
- The *Ain* goes on to give a detailed picture of the *sarkars* below the *suba.*

  This it does in the form of tables, which have eight columns giving the following information:

  1. *parganat/mahal*
  2. *qila* (forts)
  3. *arazi* and *zamin-i paimuda* (measured area)
  4. *naqdi,* revenue assessed in cash
  5. *suyurghal,* grants of revenue in charity
  6. zamindars
  7. columns 7 and 8 contain details of the castes of these zamindars*,* and their troops including their horsemen (*sawar*), foot-soldiers (*piyada*) and elephants (*fil*).

- The *mulk-abadi* gives a fascinating, detailed and highly complex view of agrarian society in northern India.
- The fourth and fifth books (*daftars*) deal with the religious, literary and cultural traditions of the people of India and also contain a collection of Akbar's "auspicious sayings".

Exercise

Level – 1

1. Sarkars, parganas and mahals *were the* administrative and fiscal divisions of

(a) Jama   (b) Subas

(c) Arazi   (d) None of the following

2. What were the most frequently cultivated crops in the sixteenth-seventeenth centuries

(a) rice   (b) wheat

(c) millets   (d) all of the above

3. Ain-i Akbari was written by

(a) Abu'l Fazl   (b) Nadir Shah

(c) Ahmad Shah   (d) Sayyid Brothers

4. Areas which received 40 inches or more of rainfall a year were generally producing

(a) Rice   (b) Wheat

(c) Millets   (d) Jute

5. Shahnahr, a canal in the Punjab got repaired during the reign of which of the following rulers?

(a) Shah Jahan   (b) Akbar

(c) Sher Shah Suri   (d) Babur

6. The zamindars held extensive personal lands termed as

(a) milkiyat   (b) paiks

(c) kharbandi   (d) None of the above

7. Giovanni Careri came from which of the following countries?

(a) Italy   (b) Portugal

(c) Spain   (d) Egypt

8. The Lohanis tribes who were engaged in overland trade, between India and Afghanistan belongs to which of the following regions

(a) Uttarakhand   (b) Himachal Pradesh

(c) Punjab   (d) Jammu and Kashmir

9. The Ahom kings had their *paiks*, people who were obliged to render military service in exchange for land.

The Ahom kings were prevalent in which of the following regions?

(a) Arunachal Pradesh

(b) Assam

(c) Manipur

(d) Nagaland

10. In Mughal empire 'jins-i kamil' represents what kind of crops?

(a) Summer crops   (b) Winter crops

(c) Perfect crops   (d) Both a and b

11. Maize was introduced into India from which of the following countries?

(a) Africa   (b) Portugal

(c) Spain   (d) Both (a) and (c)

12. The term which was used most frequently in Indo-Persian sources of the Mughal period to denote a peasant was

(a) raiyat   (b) muzarian

(c) asamis   (d) both (a) and (b)

Level – 2

13. khud-kashta and pahi-kashta were two kinds of _______.

(a) zamindars

(b) peasants

(c) cropping seasons

(d) halalkhoran

14. What were the factors that led to the constant expansion of agriculture in sixteenth-seventeenth centuries?

(a) abundance of land

(b) available labour

(c) proper irrigation supply

(d) Both a and b

15. In Mughal Empire, an official responsible for ensuring that imperial regulations were carried out in the provinces was known as

(a) Ming

(b) Safavid

(c) mansabdars

(d) Amin

16. Find the true statement about Ain-i Akbari

(a) It was part of a larger project of history writing, known as the *Akbar Nama*

(b) *Akbar Nama,* comprised three books and the *Ain-i Akbari* was the first book of that series

(c) It was organised as a compendium of imperial regulations and a gazetteer of the empire.

(d) Both (a) and (c)

17. Find the true statement about mansabdari system

    (a) It was responsible for looking after the civil affairs of the state only

    (b) All mansabdars were paid in cash

    (c) Mansabdars were transferred periodically.

    (d) None of the above

18. Find the correct statement

    (a) *Pargana* was an administrative division of a Mughal province.

    (b) *Peshkash* was a form of tribute collected by the Zamindars

    (c) Both (a) and (b)

    (d) None of the above

19. The *Ain* is made up of five books, which of the following is not the part of those five books

    (a) zamin-i paimuda

    (b) suyurghamanzil-abadi

    (c) manzil-abadi

    (d) sipah-abadi

20. In the Mughal state, the role of amil-guzar was to

    (a) Measure cultivated and cultivable lands

    (b) collect revenue

    (c) to do administrative service

    (d) None of the above

21. Find the incorrect statements regarding the classification of the lands in Mughal empire regime

    (a) Polaj is land which is annually cultivated

    (b) Parauti is land left out of cultivation for a time that it may recover its strength.

    (c) Chachar is land that has lain fallow for three or four years.

    (d) Banjar is land uncultivated for ten years and more

22. Find the incorrect statement with reference to the production of Cash crops in Mughal state

    (a) The Mughal state encouraged peasants to cultivate such crops

    (b) Cotton was grown over central India and the Deccan plateau

    (c) Bengal was famous for Jute production

    (d) Cash crops also include various sorts of oilseeds

23. The panchayat was headed by a headman known as

    (a) mandal   (b) Jagir

    (c) Mandala   (d) None of the above

24. The intermediate pastoral and fishing castes like the Sadgops and Kaivartas acquired the status of peasants in which of the following regions?

    (a) Western Region   (b) Northern Region

    (c) Eastern Region   (d) Both (a) and (b)

Answers

Level-1

1. (b)   **2.** (d)   **3.** (a)   **4.** (a)   **5.** (a)   **6.** (a)   **7.** (a)   **8.** (c)   **9.** (b)   **10.** (c)

11. (d)   **12.** (d)

Level-2

13. (b)   **14.** (d)   **15.** (d)   **16.** (d)   **17.** (c)   **18.** (d)   **19.** (b)   **20.** (b)   **21.** (d)   **22.** (c)

23. (a)   **24.** (c)

Explanations

Level – 1

1. b • *Subas and* their administrative and fiscal divisions (*sarkars*, *parganas* and *mahals*)

2. d • Since the primary purpose of agriculture is to feed people, basic staples such as rice, wheat or millets were the most frequently cultivated crops.

3. a • The *Ain-i Akbari* was the culmination of a large historical, administrative project of classification undertaken by Abu'l Fazl at the order of Emperor Akbar.

4. a • Areas which received 40 inches or more of rainfall a year were generally rice-producing zones, followed by wheat and millets, corresponding to a descending scale of precipitation.

5. a • Irrigation projects received state support as well (eg. digging of new canals (*nahr, nala*) and repairing old ones like the *shahnahr* in the Punjab during Shah Jahan's reign

6. a • The zamindars held extensive personal lands termed *milkiyat,* meaning property. *Milkiyat* lands were cultivated for the private use of zamindars, often with the help of hired or servile labour.

7. a • The testimony of an Italian traveller, Giovanni Careri, who passed through India *c.* 1690, provides a graphic account about the way silver travelled across the globe to reach India.

8. c • Tribes, like the Lohanis in the Punjab, were engaged in overland trade, between India and Afghanistan

9. b • In Assam, the Ahom kings had their *paiks*, people who were obliged to render military service in exchange for land.

• The capture of wild elephants was declared a royal monopoly by the Ahom kings.

10. c • The Mughal state also encouraged peasants to cultivate such crops as they brought in more revenue. Crops such as cotton and sugarcane were *jins-i kamil.* (literally, perfect crops) par excellence.

• Cotton was grown over a great swathe of territory spread over central India and the Deccan plateau, whereas Bengal was famous for its sugar.

• Such cash crops would also include various sorts of oilseeds (for example, mustard) and lentils.

11. d • Maize (*makka*), was introduced into India via Africa and Spain and by the seventeenth century it was being listed as one of the major crops of western India.

12. d • The term which Indo-Persian sources of the Mughal period most frequently used to denote a peasant was raiyat or muzarian.

Level – 2

13. b • Sources of the seventeenth century refer to two kinds of peasants – khud-kashta and pahi-kashta.

• khud-kashta - were residents of the village in which they held their lands.

• pahi-kashta - were non-resident cultivators who belonged to some other village, but cultivated lands elsewhere on a contractual basis.

14. d • The abundance of land, available labour and the mobility of peasants were three factors that accounted for the constant expansion of agriculture.

15. d • *Amin* was an official responsible for ensuring that imperial regulations were carried out in the provinces.

16. d • The *Ain* was part of a larger project of history writing commissioned by Akbar. This history, known as the *Akbar Nama,* comprised three books.

• The first two provided a historical narrative.

• The *Ain-i Akbari*, the third book, was organised as a compendium of imperial regulations and a gazetteer of the empire.

17. c • The Mughal administrative system had at its apex a military- cum-bureaucratic apparatus (mansabdari) which was responsible for looking after the civil and military affairs of the state.

• Some mansabdars were paid in cash (naqdi), while the majority of them were paid through assignments of revenue (jagirs) in different regions of the empire.

• They were transferred periodically.

18. d • *Pargana* was an administrative subdivision of a Mughal province.

• *Peshkash* was a form of tribute collected by the Mughal state.

19. b
- The first book, called *manzil-abadi*
- The second book, *sipah-abadi*
- The third book, *mulk-abadi*
- The fourth and fifth books (*daftars*) deal with the religious, literary and cultural traditions of the people of India

20. b
- The land revenue arrangements consisted of two stages – first, assessment and then actual collection. The *jama* was the amount assessed, as opposed to *hasil*, the amount collected. In his list of duties of the *amil-guzar* or revenue collector, Akbar decreed that while he should strive to make cultivators pay in cash, the option of payment in kind was also to be kept open.

21. d
- The Emperor Akbar in his profound sagacity classified the lands and fixed a different revenue to be paid by each.
- Polaj is land which is annually cultivated for each crop in succession and is never allowed to lie fallow. Parauti is land left out of cultivation for a time that it may recover its strength.

- Chachar is land that has lain fallow for three or four years. Banjar is land uncultivated for five years and more.

22. c
- The Mughal state also encouraged peasants to cultivate such crops as they brought in more revenue.
- Crops such as cotton and sugarcane were *jins-i kamil* par excellence.
- Cotton was grown over a great swathe of territory spread over central India and the Deccan plateau, whereas Bengal was famous for its sugar.
- Such cash crops would also include various sorts of oilseeds (for example, mustard) and lentils.

23. a
- The panchayat was headed by a headman known as *muqaddam* or *mandal*.

24. c
- In the eastern regions, intermediate pastoral and fishing castes like the Sadgops and Kaivartas acquired the status of peasants.

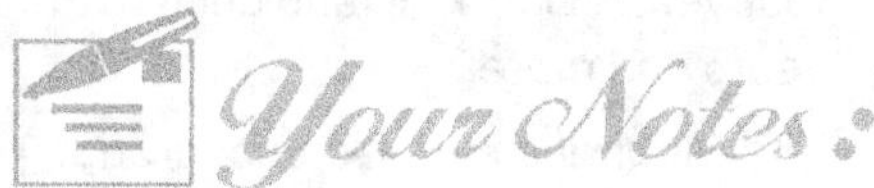 *Your Notes :* ....

CHAPTER 9

Kings and Chronicles

The Mughal Courts (c. sixteenth-seventeenth centuries)

1. The Mughals and Their Empire

- Mughals – It was not the name the rulers of the dynasty chose for themselves.

- They referred to themselves as Timurids, as descendants of the Turkish ruler Timur on the paternal side.

- During the sixteenth century, Europeans used the term Mughal to describe the Indian rulers of this branch of the family.

- The founder of the empire, Zahiruddin Babur, was driven from his Central Asian homeland, Farghana, by the warring Uzbeks.

- He first established himself at Kabul and then in 1526 pushed further into the Indian subcontinent

- His successor, Nasiruddin Humayun (1530-40, 1555-56) expanded the frontiers of the empire, but lost it to the Afghan leader Sher Shah Sur, who drove him into exile.

- Humayun took refuge in the court of the Safavid ruler of Iran.

- In 1555 Humayun defeated the Surs, but died a year later.

- Jalaluddin Akbar (1556-1605) expanded and consolidated his empire, making it the largest, strongest and richest kingdom of his time.

- Akbar succeeded in extending the frontiers of the empire to the Hindukush mountains, and checked the expansionist designs of the Uzbeks of Turan (Central Asia) and the Safavids of Iran.

- Akbar had three fairly able successors in Jahangir (1605-27), Shah Jahan (1628-58) and Aurangzeb (1658-1707), much as their characters varied.

- Imperial structure were created during the sixteenth and seventeenth centuries

- These included effective methods of administration and taxation.

- The visible centre of Mughal power was the court.

- After 1707, following the death of Aurangzeb, the power of the dynasty diminished.

- In place of the vast apparatus of empire controlled from Delhi, Agra or Lahore – the different capital cities – regional powers acquired greater autonomy.

- In 1857 the last scion of this dynasty, Bahadur Shah Zafar II, was overthrown by the British.

2. The Production of Chronicles

- Chronicles commissioned by the Mughal emperors are an important source for studying the empire and its court.

- They were written in order to project a vision of an enlightened kingdom to all those who came under its umbrella.

- The rulers wanted to ensure that there was an account of their rule for posterity.

- The histories they wrote focused on events centred on the ruler, his family, the court and nobles, wars and administrative arrangements.

- Their titles, such as the *Akbar Nama*, *Shahjahan Nama*, *Alamgir Nama*, that is, the story of Akbar, Shah Jahan and Alamgir (a title of the Mughal ruler Aurangzeb), suggest that in the eyes of their authors the history of the empire and the court was synonymous with that of the emperor.

From Turkish to Persian

- Mughal court chronicles were written in Persian.
- Under the Sultans of Delhi it flourished as a language of the court and of literary writings, alongside north Indian languages, especially Hindavi and its regional variants.
- As the Mughals were Chaghtai Turks by origin, Turkish was their mother tongue.
- Their first ruler Babur wrote poetry and his memoirs in this language.
- It was Akbar who consciously set out to make Persian the leading language of the Mughal court.
- Persian was elevated to a language of empire, conferring power and prestige on those who had a command of it.
- It was spoken by the king, the royal household and the elite at court.
- Further, it became the language of administration at all levels so that accountants, clerks and other functionaries also learnt it.
- Persian became Indianised by absorbing local idioms. A new language, Urdu, sprang from the interaction of Persian with Hindavi.
- Mughal chronicles such as the *Akbar Nama* were written in Persian, others, like Babur's memoirs, were translated from the Turkish into the Persian *Babur Nama*.
- Translations of Sanskrit texts such as the *Mahabharata* and the *Ramayana* into Persian were commissioned by the Mughal emperors.
- The *Mahabharata* was translated as the *Razmnama* (Book of Wars).

The making of manuscripts

- All books in Mughal India were manuscripts, that is, they were handwritten.
- The centre of manuscript production was the imperial *kitabkhana*.
- It is, a place where the emperor's collection of manuscripts was kept and new manuscripts were produced.
- The manuscript was seen as a precious object, a work of intellectual wealth and beauty.
- It exemplified the power of its patron, the Mughal emperor, to bring such beauty into being.
- Calligraphers and painters held a high social standing
- Calligraphy, the art of handwriting, was considered a skill of great importance.

- It was practised using different styles.
- Akbar's favourite was the *nastaliq*, a fluid style with long horizontal strokes.

3. The Painted Image

- Painters too were involved in the production of Mughal manuscripts.
- Chronicles narrating the events of a Mughal emperor's reign contained, alongside the written text, images that described an event in visual form.
- The production of paintings portraying the emperor, his court and the people who were part of it, was a source of constant tension between rulers and representatives of the Muslim orthodoxy, the *ulama*.
- Muslim rulers in many Asian regions during centuries of empire building regularly commissioned artists to paint their portraits and scenes of life in their kingdoms. (eg. the Safavid kings of Iran)

4. The Akbar Nama and the Badshah Nama

- The author of the *Akbar Nama*, Abu'l Fazl grew up in the Mughal capital of Agra.
- He was widely read in Arabic, Persian, Greek philosophy and Sufism.
- Moreover, he was a forceful debater and independent thinker who consistently opposed the views of the conservative *ulama*.
- These qualities impressed Akbar, who found Abu'l Fazl ideally suited as an adviser and a spokesperson for his policies.
- One major objective of the emperor was to free the state from the control of religious orthodoxy.
- In his role as court historian, Abu'l Fazl both shaped and articulated the ideas associated with the reign of Akbar.
- Beginning in 1589, Abu'l Fazl worked on the *Akbar Nama* for thirteen years, repeatedly revising the draft
- The *Akbar Nama* is divided into three books of which the first two are chronicles.
- The third book is the *Ain-i Akbari*.
- The first volume contains the history of mankind from Adam to one celestial cycle of Akbar's life (30 years).
- The second volume closes in the forty- sixth regnal year (1601) of Akbar.
- The very next year Abu'l Fazl fell victim to a conspiracy hatched by Prince Salim, and was murdered by his accomplice, Bir Singh Bundela.
- In the *Ain-i Akbari* the Mughal Empire is presented as having a diverse population consisting of Hindus, Jainas, Buddhists and Muslims and a composite culture.

- A pupil of Abu'l Fazl, Abdul Hamid Lahori is known as the author of the *Badshah Nama*.
- Emperor Shah Jahan commissioned him to write a history of his reign modelled on the *Akbar Nama*.
- The *Badshah Nama* is this official history in three volumes (*daftars*) of ten lunar years each.
- Lahori wrote the first and second *daftars* comprising the first two decades of the emperor's rule (1627-47); these volumes were later revised by Sadullah Khan, Shah Jahan's *wazir*.
- Infirmities of old age prevented Lahori from proceeding with the third decade which was then chronicled by the historian Waris.

5. The Ideal Kingdom

A divine light

- Abu'l Fazl placed Mughal kingship as the highest station in the hierarchy of objects receiving light emanating from God (*farr-i izadi*).
- He was inspired by a famous Iranian sufi, Shihabuddin Suhrawardi (d. 1191) who first developed this idea.
- Mughal artists, from the seventeenth century onwards, began to portray emperors wearing the halo, which they saw on European paintings to symbolise the light of God.

A unifying force

- Mughal chronicles present the empire as comprising many different ethnic and religious communities – Hindus, Jainas, Zoroastrians and Muslims.
- As the source of all peace and stability the emperor stood above all religious and ethnic groups, mediated among them, and ensured that justice and peace prevailed.
- Abu'l Fazl describes the ideal of *sulh-i kul* (absolute peace) as the cornerstone of enlightened rule.
- In *sulh-i kul* all religions and schools of thought had freedom of expression but on condition that they did not undermine the authority of the state or fight among themselves.
- The ideal of *sulh-i kul* was implemented through state policies – the nobility under the Mughals was a composite one comprising Iranis, Turanis, Afghans, Rajputs, Deccanis –
- Further, Akbar abolished the tax on pilgrimage in 1563 and *jizya* in 1564 as the two were based on religious discrimination.
- Instructions were sent to officers of the empire to follow the precept of *sulh-i kul* in administration.

Just sovereignty as social contract

- Abu'l Fazl defined sovereignty as a social contract: the emperor protects the four essences of his subjects, namely, life (*jan*), property (*mal*), honour (*namus*) and faith (*din*), and in return demands obedience and a share of resources.
- Only just sovereigns were thought to be able to honour the contract with power and Divine guidance.

6. Capitals and Courts

Capital cities

- The capital cities of the Mughals frequently shifted during the sixteenth and seventeenth centuries.
- Babur took over the Lodi capital of Agra, though during the four years of his reign the court was frequently on the move.
- During the 1560s Akbar had the fort of Agra constructed with red sandstone quarried from the adjoining regions.
- In the 1570s he decided to build a new capital, Fatehpur Sikri.
- Sikri was located on the direct road to Ajmer, where the *dargah* of Shaikh Muinuddin Chishti had become an important pilgrimage centre.
- The Mughal emperors entered into a close relationship with sufis of the Chishti *silsila*.
- Akbar commissioned the construction of a white marble tomb for Shaikh Salim Chishti next to the majestic Friday mosque at Sikri.
- The enormous arched gateway (Buland Darwaza) was meant to remind visitors of the Mughal victory in Gujarat.
- In 1585 the capital was transferred to Lahore to bring the north-west under greater control and Akbar closely watched the frontier for thirteen years.
- In 1648 the court, army and household moved from Agra to the newly completed imperial capital, Shahjahanabad.
- It was a new addition to the old residential city of Delhi, with the Red Fort, the Jama Masjid, a tree-lined esplanade with bazaars (Chandni Chowk) and spacious homes for the nobility.

The Mughal court

- Its centrepiece was the throne
- The *takht*, which gave physical form to the function of the sovereign as *axis mundi*.
- The canopy, a symbol of kingship in India for a millennium, was believed to separate the radiance of the sun from that of the sovereign.

- In court, status was determined by spatial proximity to the king.
- The place accorded to a courtier by the ruler was a sign of his importance in the eyes of the emperor.
- Once the emperor sat on the throne, no one was permitted to move from his position or to leave without permission.
- The forms of salutation to the ruler indicated the person's status in the hierarchy: deeper prostration represented higher status.
- The highest form of submission was *sijda* or complete prostration.
- Under Shah Jahan these rituals were replaced with *chahar taslim* and *zaminbos* (kissing the ground).
- The protocols governing diplomatic envoys at the Mughal court were equally explicit.
- The emperor began his day at sunrise with personal religious devotions or prayers, and then appeared on a small balcony, the *jharoka,* facing the east.
- Below, a crowd of people (soldiers, merchants, craftspersons, peasants, women with sick children) waited for a view, *darshan*, of the emperor.
- *Jharoka darshan* was introduced by Akbar with the objective of broadening the acceptance of the imperial authority as part of popular faith.
- After spending an hour at the *jharoka*, the emperor walked to the public hall of audience (*diwan-i am*) to conduct the primary business of his government.
- Two hours later, the emperor was in the *diwan-i khas* to hold private audiences and discuss confidential matters.
- The Mughal kings celebrated three major festivals a year: the solar and lunar birthdays of the monarch and Nauroz, the Iranian New Year on the vernal equinox.
- On his birthdays, the monarch was weighed against various commodities which were then distributed in charity.

Titles and gifts

- Grand titles were adopted by the Mughal emperors at the time of coronation or after a victory over an enemy.
- Mughal coins carried the full title of the reigning emperor with regal protocol.
- The granting of titles to men of merit was an important aspect of Mughal polity.
- The title Asaf Khan for one of the highest ministers originated with Asaf, the legendary minister of the prophet king Sulaiman (Solomon).

- The title Mirza Raja was accorded by Aurangzeb to his two highest-ranking nobles, Jai Singh and Jaswant Singh.

7. The Imperial Household

- The term "harem" is frequently used to refer to the domestic world of the Mughals.
- It originates in the Persian word *haram*, meaning a sacred place.
- The Mughal household consisted of the emperor's wives and concubines, his near and distant relatives and female servants and slaves.
- Polygamy was practised widely in the Indian subcontinent, especially among the ruling groups.
- Both for the Rajput clans as well as the Mughals marriage was a way of cementing political relationships and forging alliances.
- The gift of territory was often accompanied by the gift of a daughter in marriage.
- This ensured a continuing hierarchical relationship between ruling groups.
- It was through the link of marriage and the relationships that developed as a result that the Mughals were able to form a vast kinship network that linked them to important groups and helped to hold a vast empire together.
- In the Mughal household a distinction was maintained between wives who came from royal families (*begams*), and other wives (*aghas*) who were not of noble birth.
- After Nur Jahan, Mughal queens and princesses began to control significant financial resources.
- Shah Jahan's daughters Jahanara and Roshanara enjoyed an annual income often equal to that of high imperial *mansabdars*.

Humayun Nama

- *It was* written by Gulbadan Begum.
- Gulbadan was the daughter of Babur, Humayun's sister and Akbar's aunt.
- Gulbadan could write fluently in Turkish and Persian.

8. The Imperial Officials

Recruitment and rank

- One important pillar of the Mughal state was its corps of officers, also referred to by historians collectively as the nobility.
- The nobility was recruited from diverse ethnic and religious groups.
- The officer corps of the Mughals was described as a bouquet of flowers (*guldasta*) held together by loyalty to the emperor.

- In Akbar's imperial service, Turani and Iranian nobles were present from the earliest phase of carving out a political dominion.
- Two ruling groups of Indian origin entered the imperial service from 1560 onwards: the Rajputs and the Indian Muslims (Shaikhzadas).
- The first to join was a Rajput chief, Raja Bharmal Kachhwaha of Amber, to whose daughter Akbar got married.
- Iranians gained high offices under Jahangir, whose politically influential queen, Nur Jahan (d. 1645), was an Iranian.
- Aurangzeb appointed Rajputs to high positions, and under him the Marathas accounted for a sizeable number within the body of officers.
- All holders of government offices held ranks (*mansabs*) comprising two numerical designations: *zat* which was an indicator of position in the imperial hierarchy and the salary of the official (*mansabdar*), and *sawar* which indicated the number of horsemen he was required to maintain in service.
- In the seventeenth century, *mansabdars* of 1,000 *zat* or above ranked as nobles (*umara*, which is the plural of *amir*).
- The nobles participated in military campaigns with their armies and also served as officers of the empire in the provinces.
- The troopers maintained superior horses branded on the flank by the imperial mark (*dagh*).
- The emperor personally reviewed changes in rank, titles and official postings for all except the lowest-ranked officers.
- Akbar, who designed the *mansab* system, also established spiritual relationships with a select band of his nobility by treating them as his disciples (*murid*).
- A person wishing to join the service petitioned through a noble, who presented a *tajwiz* to the emperor.
- *Tajwiz* was a petition presented by a nobleman to the emperor, recommending that an applicant be recruited as *mansabdar*
- If the applicant was found suitable a *mansab* was granted to him.
- The *mir bakhshi* (paymaster general) stood in open court on the right of the emperor and presented all candidates for appointment or promotion
- There were two other important ministers at the centre: the *diwan-i ala* (finance minister) and *sadr-us sudur* (minister of grants or *madad-i maash*, and in charge of appointing local judges or *qazis*).

- The three ministers occasionally came together as an advisory body, but were independent of each other.
- Akbar with these and other advisers shaped the administrative, fiscal and monetary institutions of the empire.
- Nobles stationed at the court (*tainat-i rakab*) were a reserve force to be deputed to a province or military campaign.

Information and empire

- The *mir bakhshi* supervised the corps of court writers (*waqia nawis*) who recorded all applications and documents presented to the court, and all imperial orders (*farman*).
- In addition, agents (*wakil*) of nobles and regional rulers recorded the entire proceedings of the court under the heading "News from the Exalted Court" (*Akhbarat-i Darbar-i Mualla*) with the date and time of the court session (*pahar*).

Beyond the centre: provincial administration

- The division of functions established at the centre was replicated in the provinces (*subas*) where the ministers had their corresponding subordinates (*diwan, bakhshi* and *sadr*).
- The head of the provincial administration was the governor (*subadar*) who reported directly to the emperor.
- The *sarkars*, into which each *suba* was divided, often overlapped with the jurisdiction of *faujdars* (commandants) who were deployed with contingents of heavy cavalry and musketeers in districts.
- The local administration was looked after at the level of the *pargana* (sub-district) by three semi-hereditary officers, the *qanungo* (keeper of revenue records), the *chaudhuri* (in charge of revenue collection) and the *qazi*.

9. Beyond the Frontiers

The Safavids and Qandahar

- The political and diplomatic relations between the Mughal kings and the neighbouring countries of Iran and Turan hinged on the control of the frontier defined by the Hindukush mountains that separated Afghanistan from the regions of Iran and Central Asia.
- All conquerors who sought to make their way into the Indian subcontinent had to cross the Hindukush to have access to north India.
- A constant aim of Mughal policy was to ward off this potential danger by controlling strategic outposts – notably Kabul and Qandahar.

- Qandahar was a bone of contention between the Safavids and the Mughals.
- The fortress-town had initially been in the possession of Humayun, reconquered in 1595 by Akbar.
- While the Safavid court retained diplomatic relations with the Mughals, it continued to stake claims to Qandahar.
- In 1613 Jahangir sent a diplomatic envoy to the court of Shah Abbas to plead the Mughal case for retaining Qandahar, but the mission failed.
- In the winter of 1622 a Persian army besieged Qandahar.
- The ill-prepared Mughal garrison was defeated and had to surrender the fortress and the city to the Safavids.

The Ottomans: pilgrimage and trade

- The relationship between the Mughals and the Ottomans was marked by the concern to ensure free movement for merchants and pilgrims in the territories under Ottoman control.
- This was especially true for the Hijaz, that part of Ottoman Arabia where the important pilgrim centres of Mecca and Medina were located.

Jesuits at the Mughal court

- Europe received knowledge of India through the accounts of Jesuit missionaries, travellers, merchants and diplomats.
- The Jesuit accounts are the earliest impressions of the Mughal court ever recorded by European writers.
- The Portuguese king was also interested in the propagation of Christianity with the help of the missionaries of the Society of Jesus (the Jesuits).
- Akbar was curious about Christianity and dispatched an embassy to Goa to invite Jesuit priests.
- The first Jesuit mission reached the Mughal court at Fatehpur Sikri in 1580 and stayed for about two years.
- The Jesuits spoke to Akbar about Christianity and debated its virtues with the *ulama*.
- Two more missions were sent to the Mughal court at Lahore, in 1591 and 1595.

10. Questioning Formal Religion

- Akbar's quest for religious knowledge led to interfaith debates in the *ibadat khana* at Fatehpur Sikri between learned Muslims, Hindus, Jainas, Parsis and Christians.
- Akbar's religious views matured as he queried scholars of different religions and sects and gathered knowledge about their doctrines.
- Akbar moved away from the orthodox Islamic ways of understanding religions towards a self-conceived eclectic form of divine worship focused on light and the sun.
- Akbar and Abu'l Fazl created a philosophy of light and used it to shape the image of the king and ideology of the state.

Exercise

Level – 1

1. The name 'Mughals' was given by ____

(a) Timurids　　　　(b) Turkish ruler

(c) Europeans　　　 (d) British

2. Who among the following referred to themselves as Timurids, as descendants of the Turkish ruler Timur?

(a) Mughals　　　　(b) Tughlaq

(c) The Lodhi　　　 (d) Khiji

3. Who was the founder of the Mughal empire?

(a) Zahiruddin Babur

(b) Humayun

(c) Jahangir

(d) Shah Jahan

4. Consider the following description:

He expanded the frontiers of the empire, but lost it to the Afghan leader Sher Shah Sur, who drove him into exile. He took refuge in the court of the Safavid ruler of Iran. In 1555 He defeated the Surs, but died a year later.

The above statement best describes which of the following Mughal rulers?

(a) Nasiruddin Humayun

(b) Jalaluddin Akbar

(c) Jahangir

(d) Shah Jahan

5. Find the incorrect statement about Jalaluddin Akbar

(a) He made his empire, largest, strongest and richest kingdom of his time.

(b) He succeeded in extending the frontiers of the empire to the Hindukush mountains

(c) Akbar was succeeded by Shah Jahan

(d) None of the above

6. Find the true statement about the decline of Mughal dynasty?

(a) After 1707, following the death of Shah Jahan, the power of the dynasty diminished

(b) Regional powers acquired greater autonomy.

(c) In 1857 the last scion of this dynasty, Bahadur Shah Zafar II, was killed by the British.

(d) All of the above

7. Assertion (A): Chronicles commissioned by the Mughal emperors are an important source for studying the empire and its court.

Reason (R): They were written in order to project a vision of an enlightened kingdom to all those who came under its umbrella

(a) Both A and R are true, and R is the correct explanation of A.

(b) Both A and R are true, but R is not the correct explanation of A.

(c) A is true but R is false.

(d) A is false but R is true.

8. Find the odd one out

Titles	Rulers
(a) Akbar Nama.	Akbar
(b) Shahjahan Nama	Shah Jahan
(c) Alamgir Nama	Aurangzed
(d) *Humayunama*	Gulbadan Begam

9. Mughal court chronicles were written in __________

(a) Persian　　　　　(b) Chaghtai Turks

(c) Turkish　　　　　(d) Hindavi

10. The mother tongue of the Mughals was

(a) Turkish　　　　　(b) Persian

(c) Arabic　　　　　 (d) Urdu

11. Which of the following leader made Persian, the leading language of the Mughal court.

(a) Akbar　　　　　 (b) Jahangir

(c) Shah Jahan　　　(d) Aurangzeb

12. The Razmnama is a Persian translated version of which of the following books?

(a) Mahabharata　　(b) Ramayana

(c) Rig Veda　　　　(d) None of the following

Level – 2

13. Find the true statement about Mughal manuscripts

(a) All books in Mughal India were manuscripts

(b) All the books were handwritten.

(c) The centre of manuscript production was the imperial kitabkhana

(d) All of the above

14. Calligraphy is the art of __________

   (a) Painters   (b) handwriting

   (c) Traditional dance   (d) dictation

15. Who was the author of the *Akbar Nama?*

   (a) Sadullah Khan

   (b) Shah Jahan

   (c) Abu'l Fazl

   (d) Bir Singh Bundela

16. In the *Ain-i Akbari* the Mughal Empire is presented as having a diverse population consisting of

   1. Hindus

   2. Jainas

   3. Buddhists

   4. Muslims

   Choose the correct answer from the codes given below

   (a) 1, 2 and 3 only

   (b) 2, 3 and 4 only

   (c) 1, 3 and 4 only

   (d) 1, 2, 3 and 4

17. Find the true statement about Akbar Nama

   (a) Abu'l Fazl worked on the *Akbar Nama* for thirteen years

   (b) The *Akbar Nama* is divided into three books of which the first two are chronicles.

   (c) The third book of *Akbar Nama* is the *Ain-i Akbari.*

   (d) All of the above

18. Who was the author of Badshah Nama?

   (a) Abu'l Fazl   (b) Abdul Hamid Lahori

   (c) Sadullah Khan   (d) None of the above

19. Who among the following leaders abolished the tax on pilgrimage and *jizya*

   (a) Akbar   (b) Jahangir

   (c) Shah Jahan   (d) Aurangzeb

20. Jharoka *darshan* was introduced by ______________with the objective of broadening the acceptance of the imperial authority as part of popular faith.

   (a) Akbar   (b) Jahangir

   (c) Shah Jahan   (d) Aurangzeb

Answers

Level-1

1. (c)   **2.** (a)   **3.** (a)   **4.** (a)   **5.** (c)   **6.** (b)   **7.** (a)   **8.** (d)   **9.** (a)   **10.** (a)

11. (a)   **12.** (a)

Level-2

13. (d)   **14.** (b)   **15.** (c)   **16.** (d)   **17.** (d)   **18.** (b)   **19.** (a)   **20.** (a)

Explanations

Level – 1

1. c • During the sixteenth century, Europeans used the term Mughal to describe the Indian rulers of this branch of the family.

2. a • Mughals – It was not the name the rulers of the dynasty chose for themselves.

• They referred to themselves as Timurids, as descendants of the Turkish ruler Timur on the paternal side.

3. a • The founder of the empire, Zahiruddin Babur, was driven from his Central Asian homeland, Farghana, by the warring Uzbeks.

• He first established himself at Kabul and then in 1526 pushed further into the Indian subcontinent

4. a • Nasiruddin Humayun (1530-40, 1555-56) expanded the frontiers of the empire, but lost it to the Afghan leader Sher Shah Sur, who drove him into exile.

• Humayun took refuge in the court of the Safavid ruler of Iran.

• In 1555 Humayun defeated the Surs, but died a year later.

5. c • Jalaluddin Akbar (1556-1605) expanded and consolidated his empire, making it the largest, strongest and richest kingdom of his time.

• Akbar succeeded in extending the frontiers of the empire to the Hindukush mountains, and checked the expansionist designs of the Uzbeks of Turan (Central Asia) and the Safavids of Iran.

• Akbar had three fairly able successors in Jahangir (1605-27), Shah Jahan (1628-58) and Aurangzeb (1658-1707), much as their characters varied.

6. b • After 1707, following the death of Aurangzeb, the power of the dynasty diminished.

• In place of the vast apparatus of empire controlled from Delhi, Agra or Lahore – the different capital cities – regional powers acquired greater autonomy.

• In 1857 the last scion of this dynasty, Bahadur Shah Zafar II, was overthrown by the British.

7. a • Chronicles commissioned by the Mughal emperors are an important source for studying the empire and its court.

• They were written in order to project a vision of an enlightened kingdom to all those who came under its umbrella.

8. d • The histories they wrote focused on events centred on the ruler, his family, the court and nobles, wars and administrative arrangements.

• Their titles, such as the *Akbar Nama*, *Shahjahan Nama*, *Alamgir Nama*, that is, the story of Akbar, Shah Jahan and Alamgir (a title of the Mughal ruler Aurangzeb), suggest that in the eyes of their authors the history of the empire and the court was synonymous with that of the emperor.

9. a • Mughal court chronicles were written in Persian.

10. a • As the Mughals were Chaghtai Turks by origin, Turkish was their mother tongue.

• Their first ruler Babur wrote poetry and his memoirs in this language.

11. a • It was Akbar who consciously set out to make Persian the leading language of the Mughal court.

• Persian was elevated to a language of empire, conferring power and prestige on those who had a command of it.

• It was spoken by the king, the royal household and the elite at court.

12. a • The *Mahabharata* was translated as the *Razmnama* (Book of Wars).

Level – 2

13. d • All books in Mughal India were manuscripts, that is, they were handwritten.

• The centre of manuscript production was the imperial *kitabkhana*.

• It is, a place where the emperor's collection of manuscripts was kept and new manuscripts were produced.

14. b • Calligraphers and painters held a high social standing

• Calligraphy, the art of handwriting, was considered a skill of great importance.

• It was practised using different styles.

15. c • The author of the *Akbar Nama*, Abu'l Fazl grew up in the Mughal capital of Agra.

16. d

17. d

18. b • A pupil of Abu'l Fazl, Abdul Hamid Lahori is known as the author of the *Badshah Nama*.

• Emperor Shah Jahan commissioned him to write a history of his reign modelled on the *Akbar Nama*.

• The *Badshah Nama* is this official history in three volumes (*daftars*) of ten lunar years each.

• Lahori wrote the first and second *daftars* comprising the first two decades of the emperor's rule (1627-47); these volumes were later revised by Sadullah Khan, Shah Jahan's *wazir*.

19. a • Akbar abolished the tax on pilgrimage in 1563 and *jizya* in 1564 as the two were based on religious discrimination.

20. a

CHAPTER 10

Colonialism and the Countryside

Exploring Official Archives

1. Bengal and the Zamindars

- Colonial rule was first established in Bengal.
- In Bengal earliest attempts were made to reorder rural society and establish a new regime of land rights and a new revenue system.

An auction in Burdwan

- The Permanent Settlement had come into operation in 1793.
- The East India Company had fixed the revenue that each zamindar had to pay.
- The estates of those who failed to pay were to be auctioned to recover the revenue. (eg. *mahals* held by the Raja of Burdwan were being sold.)

The problem of unpaid revenue

- Over 75 per cent of the zamindaris changed hands after the Permanent Settlement.
- It was (Permanent Settlement), introduced by the British officials to resolve the problems of revenue
- By the 1770s, the rural economy in Bengal was in crisis, with recurrent famines and declining agricultural output.
- Officials felt that agriculture, trade and the revenue resources of the state could all be developed by encouraging investment in agriculture by securing rights of property and permanently fixing the rates of revenue demand.
- The Permanent Settlement was made with the rajas and *taluqdars* of Bengal.
- They were now classified as zamindars, and they had to pay the revenue demand that was fixed in perpetuity.
- In terms of this definition, the zamindar was not a landowner in the village, but a revenue Collector of the state.

- Zamindars had several (sometimes as many as 400) villages under them.
- In Company calculations the villages within one zamindari formed one revenue estate.
- The zamindar collected rent from the different villages, paid the revenue to the Company, and retained the difference as his income.
- He was expected to pay the Company regularly, failing which his estate could be auctioned.

Why zamindars defaulted on payments

- Zamindars regularly failed to pay the revenue demand and unpaid balances accumulated.

  The reasons for this failure were various.

  1. The Company pegged the revenue demand high
  2. This high demand was imposed in the 1790s, a time when the prices of agricultural produce were depressed, making it difficult for the *ryots* to pay their dues to the zamindar.
  3. The revenue was invariable, regardless of the harvest, and had to be paid punctually (*Sunset Law, if payment did not come in by sunset of the specified date, the zamindari was liable to be auctioned.*)
  4. The Permanent Settlement initially limited the power of the zamindar to collect rent from the *ryot* and manage his zamindari.

zamindars

- The Company subdue their authority and restrict their autonomy.
- The zamindars' troops were disbanded, customs duties abolished, and their "*cutcheries*" (courts) brought under the supervision of a Collector appointed by the Company.

- Zamindars lost their power to organise local justice and the local police.
- Over time the collectorate emerged as an alternative centre of authority, severely restricting what the zamindar could do.

The rise of the *jotedars*

- While many zamindars were facing a crisis at the end of the eighteenth century, a group of rich peasants were consolidating their position in the villages.
- Location - Dinajpur district in North Bengal
- By the early nineteenth century, *jotedars* had acquired vast areas of land
- They controlled local trade as well as moneylending, exercising immense power over the poorer cultivators of the region.
- A large part of their land was cultivated through sharecroppers (*adhiyars* or *bargadars*) who brought their own ploughs, laboured in the field, and handed over half the produce to the *jotedars* after the harvest.
- The power of *jotedars* was more effective than that of zamindars.
- Unlike zamindars who often lived in urban areas, *jotedars* were located in the villages and exercised direct control over a considerable section of poor villagers.
- The *jotedars* were most powerful in North Bengal
- In some places they were called *haoladars*, elsewhere they were known as *gantidars* or *mandals*.
- Their rise inevitably weakened zamindari authority.

The zamindars resist (ingenious methods they used to retain their zamindaris.)

- Faced with an exorbitantly high revenue demand and possible auction of their estates, they devised ways of surviving the pressures.
- Fictitious sale and manipulating the auctions were some of the strategies
- Between 1793 and 1801 four big zamindaris of Bengal, including Burdwan, made *benami* purchases that collectively yielded as much as Rs 30 lakh. Of the total sales at the auctions, over 15 per cent were fictitious.
- By the beginning of the nineteenth century the depression in prices was over.
- Thus those who had survived the troubles of the 1790s consolidated their power.
- Rules of revenue payment were also made somewhat flexible.

- As a result, the zamindar's power over the villages was strengthened.
- It was only during the Great Depression of the 1930s that they finally collapsed and the *jotedars* consolidated their power in the countryside.

The Fifth Report

- Many of the changes we are discussing were documented in detail in a report that was submitted to the British Parliament in 1813.
- It was the fifth of a series of reports on the administration and activities of the East India Company in India.
- It contain petitions of zamindars and *ryots*, reports of collectors from different districts, statistical tables on revenue returns, and notes on the revenue and judicial administration of Bengal and Madras
- Due to the maladministration of the company, the British Parliament passed a series of Acts in the late eighteenth century to regulate and control Company rule in India.
- It forced the Company to produce regular reports on the administration of India and appointed committees to enquire into the affairs of the Company.
- The Fifth Report was one such report produced by a Select Committee.
- It became the basis of intense parliamentary debates on the nature of the East India Company's rule in India.

2. The Hoe and the Plough

In the hills of Rajmahal

- Buchanan (an employee of the British East India Company) travelled through the Rajmahal hills in the early nineteenth century
- Buchanan's journal gives us tantalising glimpses of the hill folk of Rajmahal hills in the early nineteenth century.
- These hill folk were known as Paharias.
- They lived around the Rajmahal hills, subsisting on forest produce and practising shifting cultivation.
- They cleared patches of forest by cutting bushes and burning the undergrowth.
- On these patches, enriched by the potash from the ash, the Paharias grew a variety of pulses and millets for consumption.
- They scratched the ground lightly with hoes, cultivated the cleared land for a few years, then left it fallow so that it could recover its fertility, and moved to a new area.

- From the forests they collected *mahua* (a flower) for food, silk cocoons and resin for sale, and wood for charcoal production.
- Activities of the Paharias – as hunters, shifting cultivators, food gatherers, charcoal producers, silkworm rearers
- They considered the entire region as their land, the basis of their identity as well as survival; and they resisted the intrusion of outsiders.
- With their base in the hills, the Paharias regularly raided the plains where settled agriculturists lived.
- As settled agriculture expanded, the area under forests and pastures contracted.
- This sharpened the conflict between hill folk and settled cultivators.
- In the 1770s the British embarked on a brutal policy of extermination, hunting the Paharias down and killing them.
- Santhals were pouring into the area, clearing forests, cutting down timber, ploughing land and growing rice and cotton.
- As the lower hills were taken over by Santhal settlers, the Paharias receded deeper into the Rajmahal hills.
- If Paharia life was symbolised by the hoe, which they used for shifting cultivation, the settlers came to represent the power of the plough.
- The battle between the hoe and the plough was a long one.

The Santhals: Pioneer settlers

- Location - Ganjuria Pahar (part of the Rajmahal ranges)
- The frontiers of cultivation here had been extended by the Santhals.
- They had moved into this area around 1800, displaced the hill folk who lived on these lower slopes, cleared the forests and settled the land.

How did the Santhals reach the Rajmahal hills?

- The Santhals had begun to come into Bengal around the 1780s.
- Zamindars hired them to reclaim land and expand cultivation, and British officials invited them to settle in the Jangal Mahals.
- Having failed to subdue the Paharias and transform them into settled agriculturists, the British turned to the Santhals.

- The Paharias refused to cut forests, resisted touching the plough, and continued to be turbulent.
- The Santhals, by contrast, appeared to be ideal settlers, clearing forests and ploughing the land with vigour.
- The Santhals were given land and persuaded to settle in the foothills of Rajmahal.
- By 1832 a large area of land was demarcated as Damin-i-Koh.
- This was declared to be the land of the Santhals.
- They were to live within it, practise plough agriculture, and become settled peasants.
- The land was separated from both the world of the settled agriculturists of the plains and the Paharias of the hills.
- After the demarcation of Damin-i-Koh, Santhal settlements expanded rapidly.
- From 40 Santhal villages in the area in 1838, as many as 1,473 villages had come up by 1851.
- Over the same period, the Santhal population increased from a mere 3,000 to over 82,000.
- As cultivation expanded, an increased volume of revenue flowed into the Company's coffers.
- When the Santhals settled on the peripheries of the Rajmahal hills, the Paharias resisted but were ultimately forced to withdraw deeper into the hills.
- The Santhals, gave up their earlier life of mobility and settled down, cultivating a range of commercial crops for the market, and dealing with traders and moneylenders.
- The Santhals, however, soon found that the land they had brought under cultivation was slipping away from their hands.
- The state was levying heavy taxes on the land that the Santhals had cleared, moneylenders (*dikus*) were charging them high rates of interest
- By the 1850s, the Santhals rebelled against zamindars, moneylenders and the colonial state, in order to create an ideal world for themselves where they would rule.
- It was after the Santhal Revolt (1855-56) that the Santhal Pargana was created, carving out 5,500 square miles from the districts of Bhagalpur and Birbhum.
- The colonial state hoped that by creating a new territory for the Santhals and imposing some special laws within it, the Santhals could be conciliated.

3. A Revolt in the Countryside

The Bombay Deccan

- Through the nineteenth century, peasants in various parts of India rose in revolt against moneylenders and grain dealers.
- One such revolt occurred in 1875 in the Deccan.

Account books are burnt

- The movement began at Supa, a large village in Poona (present-day Pune) district.
- It was a market centre where many shopkeepers and moneylenders lived.
- On 12 May1875, *ryots* from surrounding rural areas gathered and attacked the shopkeepers, demanding their *bahi khatas* (account books) and debt bonds.
- They burnt the *khatas*, looted grain shops, and in some cases set fire to the houses of *sahukars*.
- Terrified of peasant attacks, the *sahukars* fled the villages, very often leaving their property and belongings behind.
- As the revolt spread, British officials saw the spectre of 1857.
- Police posts were established in villages to frighten rebellious peasants into submission.
- It took several months to bring the countryside under control.

A new revenue system

- As British rule expanded from Bengal to other parts of India, new systems of revenue were imposed.
- The Permanent Settlement was rarely extended to any region beyond Bengal.

Reasons

- **First :**As after 1810 agricultural prices rose, increasing the value of harvest produce, and enlarging the income of the Bengal zamindars.
- So in territories annexed in the nineteenth century, temporary revenue settlements were made to maximise its land revenue.
- **Second:**In Maharashtra when British officials set about formulating the terms of the early settlement in the 1820s, they operated with some of the ideas of the famous economist of 1820s David Ricardo.

Ricardo's theory

- A landowner should have a claim only to the "average rent" that prevailed at a given time.
- When the land yielded more than this "average rent", the landowner had a surplus that the state needed to tax.

- If tax was not levied, cultivators were likely to turn into rentiers, and their surplus income was unlikely to be productively invested in the improvement of the land.

Ricardo's theory in context of Bengal

- In Bengal the zamindars seemed to have turned into rentiers, leasing out land and living on the rental incomes.
- It was therefore necessary, the British officials now felt, to have a different system.

Ryotwari settlement

- The revenue system that was introduced in the Bombay Deccan came to be known as the *ryotwari* settlement.
- Unlike the Bengal system, the revenue was directly settled with the *ryot*.
- The average income from different types of soil was estimated, the revenue-paying capacity of the *ryot* was assessed and a proportion of it fixed as the share of the state.
- The lands were resurveyed every 30 years and the revenue rates increased.
- Therefore the revenue demand was no longer permanent.

Revenue demand and peasant debt

- The first revenue settlement in the Bombay Deccan was made in the 1820s.
- The revenue that was demanded was so high that in many places peasants deserted their villages and migrated to new regions.
- By the 1830s, Prices of agricultural products fell sharply after 1832 and did not recover for over a decade and a half.
- This meant a further decline in peasants' income.
- At the same time the countryside was devastated by a famine that struck in the years 1832-34.
- Unpaid balances of revenue mounted.
- In such years revenue could rarely be paid without a loan from a moneylender.
- But once a loan was taken, the *ryot* found it difficult to pay it back.
- As debt mounted, and loans remained unpaid, peasants' dependence on moneylenders increased.
- By the 1840s, officials were finding evidence of alarming levels of peasant indebtedness everywhere.
- By the mid-1840s there were signs of an economic recovery of sorts.

- The revenue demand was moderated to encourage peasants to expand cultivation.
- After 1845 agricultural prices recovered steadily.

Then came the cotton boom

- In 1857 the Cotton Supply Association was founded in Britain, and in 1859 the Manchester Cotton Company was formed.
- Their objective was "to encourage cotton production in every part of the world suited for its growth".
- India was seen as a country that could supply cotton to Lancashire if the American supply dried up.
- It possessed suitable soil, a climate favourable to cotton cultivation, and cheap labour.
- When the American Civil War broke out in 1861, raw cotton imports from America fell to less than three per cent of the normal
- These developments had a profound impact on the Deccan countryside.
- The *ryots* in the Deccan villages suddenly found access to seemingly limitless credit.
- They were being given Rs 100 as advance for every acre they planted with cotton.
- While the American crisis continued, cotton production in the Bombay Deccan expanded.
- Between 1860 and 1864 cotton acreage doubled.
- By 1862 over 90 per cent of cotton imports into Britain were coming from India.
- But these boom years did not bring prosperity to all cotton producers.
- Some rich peasants did gain, but for the large majority, cotton expansion meant heavier debt.

Credit dries up

- By 1865, the Civil War ended, cotton production in America revived and Indian cotton exports to Britain steadily declined.
- Export merchants and *sahukars* in Maharashtra were no longer keen on extending long-term credit.
- While credit dried up, the revenue demand increased.
- The first revenue settlement, as we have seen, was in the 1820s and 1830s.
- Now it was time for the next.

- And in the new settlement, the demand was increased dramatically: from 50 to 100 per cent.
- Yet again they(peasants) had to turn to the moneylender. But the moneylender now refused loans.
- He no longer had confidence in the *ryots'* capacity to repay.

The experience of injustice

- Moneylending was certainly widespread before colonial rule and moneylenders were often powerful figures.
- A variety of customary norms regulated the relationship between the moneylender and the *ryot*.
- One general norm was that the interest charged could not be more than the principal.
- This was meant to limit the moneylender's exactions and defined what could be counted as "fair interest".
- Under colonial rule this norm broke down as investigated by the Deccan Riots Commission
- The *ryots* complained of moneylenders manipulating laws and forging accounts.
- Moneylenders used a variety of other means to short-change the *ryot*: they refused to give receipts when loans were repaid, entered fictitious figures in bonds, acquired the peasants' harvest at low prices, and ultimately took over peasants' property.
- Deeds and bonds appeared as symbols of the new oppressive system.
- Over time, peasants came to associate the misery of their lives with the new regime of bonds and deeds.
- They were made to sign and put thumb impressions on documents, but they did not know what they were actually signing.
- But they had no choice because to survive they needed loans, and moneylenders were unwilling to give loans without legal bonds.

4. The Deccan Riots Commission

- The Government of Bombay to set up a commission of enquiry to investigate into the causes of the riots.
- The commission produced a report that was presented to the British Parliament in 1878.

Exercise

Level – 1

1. The first Colonial rule was established in __________

(a) Bengal   (b) Madras

(c) Bombay   (d) Surat

2. The East India Company had fixed the revenue that each zamindar had to pay. The estates of those who failed to pay were to be auctioned to recover the revenue.

The above statement best describes which of the following revenue system

(a) Mansabdari System

(b) Permanent Settlement

(c) Ryotwari Settlement

(d) None of the above

3. Find the true statement with reference to Permanent Settlement in Bengal

(a) The zamindars were the landowners in the village

(b) The taluqdars were the revenue Collector of the state.

(c) There was a single village under each zamindar

(d) The Permanent Settlement was made with the rajas and *taluqdars* of Bengal.

4. In terms of Company calculations, one revenue estate consisted of

(a) villages within a province

(b) villages within the kingdom

(c) villages within one zamindari

(d) none of the above

5. The Permanent Settlement had come into operation in __________

(a) 1893

(b) 1814

(c) 1793

(d) 1799

6. Zamindars regularly failed to pay the revenue demand because which of the following reasons?

(a) High revenue demand pegged by the company

(b) The revenue was invariable, regardless of the harvest

(c) Limited the power of the zamindar to collect rent from the *ryot*

(d) All of the above

7. After the implementation of the Permanent Settlement, the Zamindar's *cutcheries* brought under the supervision of a Collector appointed by the Company.

The literal meaning of cutcherries is

(a) asset   (b) land

(c) court   (d) custom duty

8. Find the incorrect statement about jotedars

(a) The power of *jotedars* was more effective than that of zamindars.

(b) They were a group of rich peasants

(c) *Jotedars* were located in the villages

(d) The *jotedars* were the most powerful group in entire Bengal

9. Haoladars, gantidars or mandals are some of the other names of

(a) adhiyars   (b) bargadars

(c) jotedars   (d) zamindars

10. The zamindars collapsed completely during which of the following events?

(a) Great Depression of the 1930s

(b) Permanent Settlement

(c) Sunset Laws

(d) Emergence of rajas and taluqdars of Bengal

Level – 2

11. Find the true statement about the Fifth Report produced by a Select Committee:

(a) It contain petitions of zamindars and *ryots*

(b) It forced the Company to produce regular reports on the trade and commerce of India

(c) It became the basic of intense parliamentary debates on the nature of the East India Company's rule in India.

(d) Both 1 and 3

12. Consider the following statements

They lived around the Rajmahal hills, subsisting on forest produce and practising shifting cultivation. They cleared patches of forest by cutting bushes and burning the undergrowth. On these patches, they grew a variety of pulses and millets for consumption.

The above statement best describes which of the following section of people

(a) Mahua   (b) Paharias

(c) Santhals   (d) Both a and b

13. The revenue system that was introduced in the Bombay Deccan came to be known as the

(a) Ryotwari settlement.

(b) Permanent settlement

(c) Mansabdari

(d) None of the above

14. Find the correct statement about the Ryotwari settlement

(a) The revenue was directly settled with the *ryot*.

(b) The revenue demand was permanent.

(c) The lands were resurveyed every 30

(d) Both a and c

15. Assertion (A): The Permanent Settlement was rarely extended to any region beyond Bengal

Reason (R): As British rule expanded from Bengal to other parts of India, new systems of revenue were imposed.

(a) Both A and R are true, and R is the correct explanation of A.

(b) Both A and R are true, but R is not the correct explanation of A.

(c) A is true but R is false.

(d) A is false but R is true.

16. By 1832, a large area of land was demarcated as Damin-i-Koh. This was declared to be the land of the ________________

(a) Santhals.   (b) Paharias

(c) Daiku   (d) Peasants

17. The Santhals were given land and were persuaded to settle in the foothills of

(a) Rajmahal hills

(b) Chotanagpur

(c) Vidhyan range

(d) None of the above

18. The Government of Bombay set up a commission of enquiry to investigate into the causes of the ________

(a) The Deccan Riots

(b) Santhals rebellion

(c) Paharias invasion

(d) Daiku intrusion

19. Find the true statement with reference to the cotton production in India during the mid-nineteen century

(a) The *ryots* in the Deccan villages witness the expansion of cotton production

(b) The raw cotton imports from America to Britain fell to less than three per cent of the normal

(c) By 1862 over 90 per cent of cotton imports into Britain were coming from India.

(d) All of the above

20. Deeds and bonds appeared as symbols of the new oppressive system for which of the following section of people?

(a) Moneylenders

(b) Peasants

(c) Ryots

(d) Santhals

Answers

Level-1

1. (a)	2. (b)	3. (d)	4. (c)	5. (c)	6. (d)	7. (c)	8. (d)	9. (c)	10. (a)

Level-2

11. (d)	12. (b)	13. (a)	14. (d)	15. (a)	16. (a)	17. (a)	18. (a)	19. (d)	20. (b)

Explanations

Level – 1

1. a

2. b

3. d • The Permanent Settlement was made with the rajas and *taluqdars* of Bengal.
  • They were now classified as zamindars, and they had to pay the revenue demand that was fixed in perpetuity.
  • In terms of this definition, the zamindar was not a landowner in the village, but a revenue Collector of the state.
  • Zamindars had several (sometimes as many as 400) villages under them.

4. c • In Company calculations the villages within one zamindari formed one revenue estate.
  • The zamindar collected rent from the different villages, paid the revenue to the Company, and retained the difference as his income.

5. c

6. d zamindars

7. c • The zamindars' troops were disbanded, customs duties abolished, and their "*cutcheries*" (courts) brought under the supervision of a Collector appointed by the Company.

8. d • Unlike zamindars who often lived in urban areas, *jotedars* were located in the villages and exercised direct control over a considerable section of poor villagers.
  • The *jotedars* were most powerful in North Bengal

9. c • In some places jotedars were called *haoladars*, elsewhere they were known as *gantidars* or *mandals*.
  • In some places they were called *haoladars*, elsewhere they were known as *gantidars* or *mandals*.
  • Their rise inevitably weakened zamindari authority.

10. a • During the Great Depression of the 1930s they collapsed and the *jotedars* consolidated their power in the countryside.

Level – 2

11. d • Due to the maladministration of the company, the British Parliament passed a series of Acts in the late eighteenth century to regulate and control Company rule in India.
  • It forced the Company to produce regular reports on the administration of India and appointed committees to enquire into the affairs of the Company.
  • The Fifth Report was one such report produced by a Select Committee.
  • It became the basis of intense parliamentary debates on the nature of the East India Company's rule in India.

12. b

13. a

14. d • Unlike the Bengal system, the revenue was directly settled with the *ryot*.
  • The average income from different types of soil was estimated, the revenue-paying capacity of the *ryot* was assessed and a proportion of it fixed as the share of the state.
  • The lands were resurveyed every 30 years and the revenue rates increased.
  • Therefore the revenue demand was no longer permanent.

15. a

16. a • By 1832 a large area of land was demarcated as Damin-i-Koh.
  • This was declared to be the land of the Santhals.

17. a • Having failed to subdue the Paharias and transform them into settled agriculturists, the British turned to the Santhals.
  • The Santhals, by contrast, appeared to be ideal settlers, clearing forests and ploughing the land with vigour.
  • The Santhals were given land and persuaded to settle in the foothills of Rajmahal.

18. a • The Government of Bombay set up a commission of enquiry to investigate into the causes of the riots.
  • The commission produced a report that was presented to the British Parliament in 1878.

19. d • When the American Civil War broke out in 1861, raw cotton imports from America fell to less than three per cent of the normal
  • The *ryots* in the Deccan villages suddenly found access to seemingly limitless credit.
  • Between 1860 and 1864 cotton acreage doubled.
  • By 1862 over 90 per cent of cotton imports into Britain were coming from India.

20. b • Moneylenders used a variety of other means to short-change the *ryot*: they refused to give receipts when loans were repaid, entered fictitious figures in bonds, acquired the peasants' harvest at low prices, and ultimately took over peasants' property.
  • Deeds and bonds appeared as symbols of the new oppressive system.
  • Over time, peasants came to associate the misery of their lives with the new regime of bonds and deeds.
  • They were made to sign and put thumb impressions on documents, but they did not know what they were actually signing.

CHAPTER 11

Rebels and the Raj

The Revolt of 1857 and Its Representations

1. Pattern of the Rebellion

How the mutinies began

- Signals used by the sepoys to began their action: firing of the evening gun or the sounding of the bugle.
- They first seized the bell of arms and plundered the treasury.
- They then attacked government buildings – the jail, treasury, telegraph office, record room, bungalows – burning all records.
- Everything and everybody connected with the white man became a target.
- Proclamations in Hindi, Urdu and Persian were put up in the cities calling upon the population, both Hindus and Muslims, to unite, rise and exterminate the *firangis*.
- In major towns like Lucknow, Kanpur and Bareilly, money- lenders and the rich also became the objects of rebel wrath.
- Peasants not only saw them as oppressors but also as allies of the British.
- The mutiny in the sepoy ranks quickly became a rebellion.

Terminologies

Mutiny– a collective disobedience of rules and regulations within the armed forces

Revolt – a rebellion of people against established authority and power. The terms 'revolt' and 'rebellion' can be used synonymously.

Lines of communication

- Similarity in the pattern of the revolt in different places signifies that there was communication, planning and coordination between the sepoy lines of various cantonments.

Leaders and followers

- One of the first acts of the sepoys of Meerut, was to rush to Delhi and appeal to the old Mughal emperor (Bahadur Shah) to accept the leadership of the revolt.
- Elsewhere, similar scenes were enacted though on a minor scale.
- In Kanpur, the sepoys and the people of the town gave Nana Sahib, the successor to Peshwa Baji Rao II
- In Jhansi, the rani was forced by the popular pressure around her to assume the leadership of the uprising.
- So was Kunwar Singh, a local zamindar in Arrah in Bihar.
- In Awadh, the people, in Lucknow celebrated the fall of British rule by hailing Birjis Qadr, the young son of the Nawab, as their leader.
- Elsewhere, local leaders emerged, urging peasants, zamindars and tribals to revolt.
- Shah Mal mobilised the villagers of pargana Barout in Uttar Pradesh; Gonoo, a tribal cultivator of Singhbhum in Chotanagpur, became a rebel leader of the Kol tribals of the region.

Rumours and prophecies

- The rumour that the new cartridges were greased with the fat of cows and pigs spread like wildfire across the sepoy lines of North India.
- This was not the only rumour that was circulating in North India at the beginning of 1857.
- There was the rumour that the British government had hatched a gigantic conspiracy to destroy the caste and religion of Hindus and Muslims.
- Another rumour said, the British had mixed the bone dust of cows and pigs into the flour that was sold in the market.
- There was fear and suspicion that the British wanted to convert Indians to Christianity.

Why did people believe in the rumours?

- Rumours circulate only when they resonate with the deeper fears and suspicions of people.
- The rumours in 1857 begin to make sense when seen in the context of the policies the British pursued from the late 1820s.
- British adopted policies aimed at "reforming" Indian society by introducing Western education, Western ideas and Western institutions under the leadership of Governor General Lord William Bentinck
- With the cooperation of sections of Indian society they set up English-medium schools, colleges and universities which taught Western sciences and the liberal arts.
- The British established laws to abolish customs like sati (1829) and to permit the remarriage of Hindu widows.
- The British annexed not only Awadh, but many other kingdoms and principalities like Jhansi and Satara.
- The British introduced their own system of administration, their own laws and their own methods of land settlement and land revenue collection.
- The cumulative impact of all this on the people of North India was profound.
- It seemed to the people that all that they cherished and held sacred was being destroyed and replaced by a system that was more impersonal, alien and oppressive.
- This perception was aggravated by the activities of Christian missionaries.
- In such a situation of uncertainty, rumours spread with remarkable swiftness.

2. Awadh in Revolt

- The Subsidiary Alliance had been imposed on Awadh in 1801.
- By the terms of this alliance the Nawab had to disband his military force, allow the British to position their troops within the kingdom, and act in accordance with the advice of the British Resident who was now to be attached to the court.
- The Nawab became increasingly dependent on the British to maintain law and order within the kingdom.
- He could no longer assert control over the rebellious chiefs and *taluqdars*.
- By the early 1850s, all the major areas of India had been conquered: the Maratha lands, the Doab, the Carnatic, the Punjab and Bengal.

- In 1856, the Awadh kingdom was annexed to the British Empire and Nawab Wajid Ali Shah dethroned and exiled to Calcutta.
- The removal of the Nawab led to the dissolution of the court and its culture.

The taluqdars

- The annexation also dispossessed the *taluqdars* of the region.
- Before the coming of the British, *taluqdars* maintained armed retainers, built forts, and enjoyed a degree of autonomy
- They accepted the suzerainty of the Nawab and paid the revenue of their *taluqs*.
- Immediately after the annexation, the *taluqdars* were disarmed and their forts destroyed.
- After annexation, the first British revenue settlement, known as the Summary Settlement of 1856
- The Summary Settlement proceeded to remove the *taluqdars* wherever possible.
- The dispossession of *taluqdars* meant the breakdown of an entire social order.
- The ties of loyalty and patronage that had bound the peasant to the *taluqdar* were disrupted.
- In areas like Awadh where resistance during 1857 was intense and long lasting, the fighting was carried out by *taluqdars* and their peasants.
- Many of these *taluqdars* were loyal to the Nawab of Awadh, and they joined Begum Hazrat Mahal (the wife of the Nawab) in Lucknow to fight the British; some even remained with her in defeat.

Relationship of the sepoys with their superior white officers

- In the 1820s, it was a friendly relations between the sepoys and white officers
- In the 1840s, the officers developed a sense of superiority and started treating the sepoys as their racial inferiors
- The distance between sepoys and officers grew.
- All these activities were communicated back to the villages.
- This link between the sepoys and the rural world had important implications in the course of the uprising.
- The grievances of the peasants were carried over into the sepoy lines since a vast majority of the sepoys were recruited from the villages of Awadh.
- Links existed between the sepoys and the rural world of North India.

- The large majority of the sepoys of the Bengal Army were recruited from the villages of Awadh and eastern Uttar Pradesh.
- When the sepoys defied their superior officers and took up arms they were joined very swiftly by their brethren in the villages.
- Everywhere, peasants poured into towns and joined the soldiers and the ordinary people of the towns in collective acts of rebellion.

3. What the Rebels Wanted

The vision of unity

- The rebel proclamations in 1857 repeatedly appealed to all sections of the population, irrespective of their caste and creed.
- Many of the proclamations were issued by Muslim princes or in their names but even these took care to address the sentiments of Hindus.
- The rebellion was seen as a war in which both Hindus and Muslims had equally to lose or gain.
- The proclamation that was issued under the name of Bahadur Shah appealed to the people to join the fight under the standards of both Muhammad and Mahavir.
- It was remarkable that during the uprising religious divisions between Hindus and Muslim were hardly noticeable despite British attempts to create such divisions.

Against the symbols of oppression

- The proclamations completely rejected everything associated with British rule.
- They condemned the British for the annexations they had carried out and the treaties they had broken.

- The proclamations expressed the widespread fear that the British were bent on destroying the caste and religions of Hindus and Muslims and converting them to Christianity.

The search for alternative power

- Once British rule had collapsed, the rebels in places like Delhi, Lucknow and Kanpur tried to establish some kind of structure of authority and administration.
- This was, of course, short-lived but the attempts show that the rebel leadership wanted to restore the pre-British world of the eighteenth century.
- The administrative structures established by the rebels were primarily aimed at meeting the demands of war. However, in most cases these structures could not survive the British onslaught.
- But in Awadh, where resistance to the British lasted longest.

4. Repression

- In 1857 the British did not have an easy time in putting down the rebellion.
- The whole of North India put under martial law but military officers and ordinary Britons were given the power to try and punish Indians suspected of rebellion.
- The ordinary processes of law and trial were suspended and it was put out that rebellion would have only one punishment – death.
- British attempts to recover Delhi began in earnest in early June 1857 but it was only in late September that the city was finally captured.
- The Ganegtic plain area was brought under control only in March 1858 after protracted fighting.

Exercise

Level – 1

1. A collective disobedience of rules and regulations within the armed forces called as

(a) Revolt   (b) Mutiny

(c) Rebellion   (d) None of the above

2. One of the first acts of the sepoys of Meerut, was to rush to Delhi and appeal to the old Mughal emperor _______________ to accept the leadership of the revolt.

(a) Hashim ud-Daula   (b) Bahadur Shah

(c) Siraj ud-Daulah   (d) Alivardi Khan

3. Find the incorrect statement with reference to the Pattern of the Rebellion

(a) Only white man was the target of sepoys

(b) Both Hindus and Muslims, united, rose and exterminated the British.

(c) Proclamations in Hindi, Urdu and Persian were put up in the cities calling upon the population

(d) Money- lenders and the rich also became the objects of rebel wrath.

4. In Kanpur, the sepoys and the people of the town gave Nana Sahib, the successor to__________

(a) Peshwa Baji Rao II   (b) Peshwa Baji Rao I

(c) Baji Rao I   (d) None of the above

5. In which of the following regions the people celebrated the fall of British rule by hailing Birjis Qadr, the young son of the Nawab, as their leader.

(a) Lucknow   (b) Ujjain

(c) Buxar   (d) Bareilly

6. Gonoo, a tribal cultivator of Singhbhum in Chotanagpur, became a rebel leader of the Kol tribals of the region.

The Kol tribal people belongs to which of the following states of India

(a) Jharkhand   (b) Andhra Pradesh

(c) Chhattisgarh   (d) Telangana

7. British adopted policies aimed at "reforming" Indian society by introducing Western education, Western ideas and Western institutions under the leadership of _________________

(a) William Bentinck   (b) Warren Hastings

(c) Lord Cornwallis   **(d) Lord Hastings**

8. The British established laws to abolish customs like sati in ___________ and to permit the remarriage of Hindu widows.

(a) 1829   (b) 1831

(c) 1838   (d) 1828

9. The British annexed which of the following territories?

(a) Awadh   (b) Jhansi

(c) Satara.   (d) All of the above

10. The Subsidiary Alliance was imposed on Awadh in _______

(a) 1801.   (b) 1802

(c) 1803   (d) 1804

Level – 2

11. By the terms of this alliance the Nawab had to disband his military force, allow the British to position their troops within the kingdom, and act in accordance with the advice of the British Resident who was now to be attached to the court.

The above statement describes which of the following alliances

(a) Subsidiary alliance   (b) Strategic Alliance.

(c) Doctrine of lapse   (d) Both a and c

12. In 1856, Nawab Wajid Ali Shah dethroned and exiled to Calcutta by the British Empire Nawab Wajid Ali Shah was the ruler of which of the following kingdom?

(a) Awadh   (b) Lucknow

(c) Tuglakabad   (d) Kanpur

13. After annexing Awadh, the first British revenue settlement, known as the Summary Settlement of 1856 proceeded to remove the ___________

(a) mansabdars   (b) taluqdars

(c) Zamindars   (d) Peasants

14. After the annexation of Awadh, the taluqdars of the region joined who among the following leaders to fight the British

(a) Begum Hazrat Mahal   (b) Veer Kuwar Singh

(c) Rani Laxmi Bai   (d) Tatya tope

15. The large majority of the sepoys of the Bengal Army were recruited from the villages of

1. Awadh

2. Eastern Uttar Pradesh.

3. Punjab

4. Sindh

Choose the correct answer from the codes given below

(a) 1 and 2 only   (b) 1 2 3 and 4

(c) 1 3 and 4 only   (d) 2 3 and 4 only

16. In which of the following kingdoms, the resistance to the British lasted for the longest duration?

(a) Awadh   (b) Lucknow

(c) Arrah   (d) Ballia

Answers

Level-1

1. (b)	**2.** (b)	**3.** (a)	**4.** (a)	**5.** (a)	**6.** (a)	**7.** (a)	**8.** (a)	**9.** (d)	**10.** (a)

Level-2

11. (a)	**12.** (a)	**13.** (b)	**14.** (a)	**15.** (a)	**16.** (a)

Explanations

Level – 1

1. b • Mutiny– a collective disobedience of rules and regulations within the armed forces

2. b

3. a • Signals used by the sepoys to began their action: firing of the evening gun or the sounding of the bugle.

• They first seized the bell of arms and plundered the treasury.

• They then attacked government buildings – the jail, treasury, telegraph office, record room, bungalows – burning all records.

• Everything and everybody connected with the white man became a target.

4. a • In Kanpur, the sepoys and the people of the town gave Nana Sahib, the successor to Peshwa Baji Rao II

5. a • In Awadh, the people, in Lucknow celebrated the fall of British rule by hailing Birjis Qadr, the young son of the Nawab, as their leader.

6. a

7. a • British adopted policies aimed at "reforming" Indian society by introducing Western education, Western ideas and Western institutions under the leadership of Governor General Lord William Bentinck

8. a • The British established laws to abolish customs like sati (1829) and to permit the remarriage of Hindu widows.

9. d

10. a • The Subsidiary Alliance had been imposed on Awadh in 1801.

Level – 2

11. a

12. a • In 1856, the Awadh kingdom was annexed to the British Empire and Nawab Wajid Ali Shah dethroned and exiled to Calcutta

• The removal of the Nawab led to the dissolution of the court and its culture

13. b • Immediately after the annexation of Awadh , the *taluqdars* were disarmed and their forts destroyed.

• After annexation, the first British revenue settlement, known as the Summary Settlement of 1856

• The Summary Settlement proceeded to remove the *taluqdars* wherever possible.

14. a • Many of these *taluqdars* were loyal to the Nawab of Awadh, and they joined Begum Hazrat Mahal (the wife of the Nawab) in Lucknow to fight the British; some even remained with her in defeat.

15. a • Links existed between the sepoys and the rural world of North India.

• The large majority of the sepoys of the Bengal Army were recruited from the villages of Awadh and eastern Uttar Pradesh.

16. a • In Awadh, where resistance to the British lasted longest

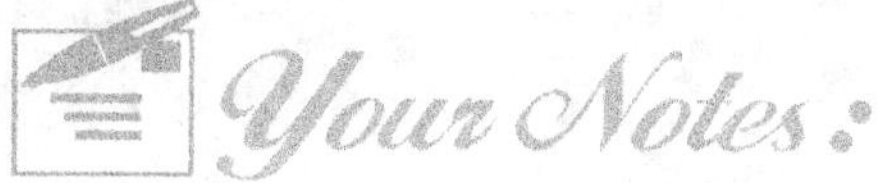
Your Notes :

THEME TWELVE

Colonial Cities

Urbanisation, Planning and Architecture

1. Towns and Cities in Pre-colonial Times

- Towns represent specific forms of economic activities and cultures.
- In the countryside people subsisted by cultivating land, foraging in the forest, or rearing animals.
- Towns by contrast were peopled with artisans, traders, administrators and rulers.
- Towns dominated over the rural population, thriving on the surplus and taxes derived from agriculture.
- Towns and cities were often fortified by walls which symbolised their separation from the countryside.
- During the sixteenth and seventeenth centuries the towns built by the Mughals like Agra, Delhi and Lahore were important centres of imperial administration and control.
- *Mansabdars* and *jagirdars* who were assigned territories in different parts of the empire usually maintained houses in these cities
- The focus of the town was oriented towards the palace and the principal mosque.
- In the towns of South India such as Madurai and Kanchipuram the principal focus was the temple.
- Medieval towns were places where everybody was expected to know their position in the social order dominated by the ruling elite. (eg. the imperial officer of North India – *kotwali,* who oversaw the internal affairs and policing of the town.

Changes in the Eighteenth Century

- The gradual erosion of Mughal power led to the demise of towns associated with their rule.
- The Mughal capitals, Delhi and Agra, lost their political authority.
- The growth of new regional powers was reflected in the increasing importance of regional capitals – Lucknow, Hyderabad, Seringapatam, Poona ,Nagpur, Baroda and Tanjore .

- Traders, administrators, artisans and others migrated from the old Mughal centres to these new capitals in search of work and patronage.
- The European commercial Companies had set up base in different places early during the Mughal era: the Portuguese in Panaji in 1510, the Dutch in Masulipatnam in 1605, the British in Madras in 1639 and the French in Pondicherry in1673.
- With the expansion of commercial activity, towns grew around these trading centres.
- By the end of the eighteenth century the land-based empires in Asia were replaced by the powerful sea-based European empires.
- As the British gradually acquired political control after the Battle of Plassey in 1757, and the trade of the English East India Company expanded, colonial port cities such as Madras, Calcutta and Bombay rapidly emerged as the new economic capitals.

2. Finding Out about Colonial Cities

Colonial records and urban history

- To keep track of life in the growing cities, the British carried out regular surveys, gathered statistical data, and published various official reports.
- When towns began to grow, maps were prepared to plan the development of towns and to develop commerce and consolidate power.
- From the late nineteenth century the British tried to raise money for administering towns through the systematic annual collection of municipal taxes.
- By the mid-nineteenth century several local censuses had been carried out in different regions. The first all-India census was attempted in 1872.
- Thereafter, from 1881, decennial (conducted every ten years) censuses became a regular feature.

Trends of change

- After 1800, urbanisation in India was sluggish.
- All through the nineteenth century up to the first two decades of the twentieth, the proportion of the urban population to the total population in India was extremely low and had remained stagnant.
- In the forty years between 1900 and 1940 the urban population increased from about 10 per cent of the total population to about 13 per cent.
- The smaller towns had little opportunity to grow economically.
- Calcutta, Bombay and Madras on the other hand grew rapidly and soon became sprawling cities.
- The growth of these three cities as the new commercial and administrative centres was at the expense of other existing urban centres.
- In eighteenth and nineteenth centuries – these cities functioned as collection depots for the export of Indian manufactures such as cotton textiles
- After the Industrial Revolution – these cities became the entry point for British-manufactured goods and for the export of Indian raw materials.
- The nature of this economic activity sharply differentiated these colonial cities from India's traditional towns and urban settlements.
- The introduction of railways in 1853 meant a change in the fortunes of towns.
- Economic activity gradually shifted away from traditional towns which were located along old routes and rivers.

3. What Were the New Towns Like?

Ports, Forts and Centres for Services

- By the eighteenth century Madras, Calcutta and Bombay had become important ports.
- The settlements that came up here were convenient points for collecting goods.
- The English East India Company built its factories and fortified it for protection.
- In Madras, Fort St George, in Calcutta Fort William and in Bombay the Fort marked out the areas of British settlement.
- From the mid-nineteenth century the expanding network of railways linked these cities to the rest of the country.
- After the 1850s, cotton mills were set up by Indian merchants and entrepreneurs in Bombay, and European-owned jute mills were established on the outskirts of Calcutta.

- This was the beginning of modern industrial development in India.
- India never became a modern industrialised country, since discriminatory colonial policies limited the levels of industrial development.

A new urban milieu

- Colonial cities reflected the mercantile culture of the new rulers.
- Economic activity near the river or the sea led to the development of docks and *ghats.*
- Along the shore were godowns, mercantile offices, insurance agencies for shipping, transport depots, banking establishments.
- The nature of the colonial city changed further in the mid-nineteenth century.
- After the Revolt of 1857 British attitudes in India were shaped by a constant fear of rebellion.
- They felt that towns needed to be better defended
- New urban spaces (Safe enclaves) called "Civil Lines" were set up.
- White people began to live in the Civil Lines.
- Cantonments– places where Indian troops under European command were stationed – were also developed as safe enclaves.

The first hill stations

- The founding and settling of hill stations was initially connected with the needs of the British army.
- Simla was founded during the course of the Gurkha War (1815-16); the Anglo-Maratha War of 1818 led to British interest in Mount Abu; and Darjeeling was wrested from the rulers of Sikkim in 1835.
- Hill stations became strategic places for billeting troops, guarding frontiers and launching campaigns against enemy rulers.
- In 1864 the Viceroy John Lawrence officially moved his council to Simla, setting seal to the practice of shifting capitals during the hot season.
- Simla also became the official residence of the commander-in-chief of the Indian army.

Social life in the new cities

- Within the cities new social groups were formed and the old identities of people were no longer important.
- All classes of people were migrating to the big cities.
- A new public sphere of debate and discussion emerged.
- Social customs, norms and practices came to be questioned.

- Social changes did not happen with ease.
- Another new class within the cities was the labouring poor or the working class.
- Paupers from rural areas flocked to the cities in the hope of employment.

4. Segregation, Town Planning and Architecture

Madras, Calcutta and Bombay

- Madras, Calcutta and Bombay gradually developed into the biggest cities of colonial India.

Settlement and segregation in Madras

- Company first trading activity centre - port of Surat port (West Coast)
- In 1639 they constructed a trading post in Madraspatam (east coast)
- This settlement was locally known as Chenapattanam.
- The Company had purchased the right of settlement from the local Telugu lords, the Nayaks of Kalahast
- With the defeat of the French in 1761, Madras became more secure and began to grow into an important commercial town.
- Fort St George became the nucleus of the White Town where most of the Europeans lived.
- The Black Town developed outside the Fort.
- This housed weavers, artisans, middlemen and interpreters who played a vital role in the Company trade.
- In Black Town there were distinct caste-specific neighbourhoods.
- Several different communities came and settled in Madras, performing a range of economic functions.
- The *dubashes* were Indians who could speak two languages – the local language and English.
- They worked as agents and merchants, acting as intermediaries between Indian society and the British.
- They used their privileged position in government to acquire wealth.
- Their powerful position in society was established by their charitable works and patronage of temples in the Black Town.
- Vellalars, a rural caste who took advantage of the new opportunities provided by British rule.
- Brahmins started competing for similar positions in the administration after the spread of English education
- Telugu Komatis were a powerful commercial group that controlled the grain trade in the city.
- Gujarati bankers had also been present since the eighteenth century.

- Paraiyars and Vanniyars formed the labouring poor.
- The Nawab of Arcot settled in nearby Triplicane which became the nucleus of a substantial Muslim settlement.
- Mylapore and Triplicane were earlier Hindu religious centres that supported a large group of Brahmins.
- San Thome with its cathedral was the centre for Roman Catholics.
- All these settlements became part of Madras city.

Town planning in Calcutta

- In 1756, Sirajudaula, the Nawab of Bengal, attacked Calcutta and sacked the small fort which the British traders had built as their depot for goods.
- Subsequently, in 1757, when Sirajudaula was defeated in the Battle of Plassey, the East India Company decided to build a new fort, one that could not be easily attacked.
- Calcutta had grown from three villages called Sutanati, Kolkata and Govindapur.
- Around the new Fort William they left a vast open space which came to be locally known as the Maidan or *garer-math*.
- The vast open space around the Fort (which still exists) became a landmark, Calcutta's first significant town planning measure.
- In 1798, Lord Wellesley became the Governor General. He built a massive palace, Government House
- After Wellesley's departure the work of town planning was carried on by the Lottery Committee (1817) with the help of the government.
- The Lottery Committee was so named because funds for town improvement were raised through public lotteries.
- The existing racial divide of the "White Town" and "Black Town" was reinforced by the new divide of "healthy" and "unhealthy".

Architecture in Bombay

- Bombay was initially seven islands.
- As the population grew, the islands were joined to create more space and they gradually fused into one big city.
- Bombay was the commercial capital of colonial India.
- As the premier port on the western coast it was the centre of international trade.
- By the end of the nineteenth century, half the imports and exports of India passed through Bombay.
- One important item of this trade was opium that the East India Company exported to China.

- It made the Company profitable and led to the growth of an Indian capitalist class.
- Bombay's capitalists came from diverse communities such as Parsi, Marwari, Konkani Muslim, Gujarati Bania, Bohra, Jew and Armenian.
- As Bombay's economy grew, many new buildings were constructed at this time.
- The architectural style was usually European.
- Initially, these buildings were at odds with the traditional Indian buildings.
- Gradually, Indians too got used to European architecture and made it their own.
- The British in turn adapted some Indian styles to suit their needs.
- For pubic buildings three broad architectural styles were used.
- Two of these were direct imports from fashions prevalent in England.
- The first was called **neo-classical or the new classical.**
- Its characteristics included construction of geometrical structures fronted with lofty pillars
- It was derived from a style that was originally typical of buildings in ancient Rome, and was subsequently revived, re-adapted and made popular during the European Renaissance.
- The Town Hall in Bombay was built in this style in 1833.
- Another group of commercial buildings, built during the cotton boom of the 1860s, was the Elphinstone Circle.

- Another style that was extensively used was the **neo-Gothic,** characterised by high-pitched roofs, pointed arches and detailed decoration.
- The Gothic style had its roots in buildings, especially churches, built in northern Europe during the medieval period.
- The neo-Gothic or new Gothic style was revived in the mid-nineteenth century in England.
- This was the time when the government in Bombay was building its infrastructure and this style was adapted for Bombay.
- An impressive group of buildings facing the seafront including the Secretariat, University of Bombay and High Court were all built in this style.
- However, the most spectacular example of the neo-Gothic style is the Victoria Terminus, the station and headquarters of the Great Indian Peninsular Railway Company.
- Towards the beginning of the twentieth century a new hybrid architectural style developed which combined the Indian with the European.
- This was called **Indo-Saracenic. "Indo"** was shorthand for Hindu and "Saracen" was a term Europeans used to designate Muslim.
- The inspiration for this style was medieval buildings in India with their domes, *chhatris*, *jalis*, arches.
- The Gateway of India, built in the traditional Gujarati style to welcome King George V and Queen Mary to India in 1911, is the most famous example of this style.
- The industrialist Jamsetji Tata built the Taj Mahal Hotel in a similar style.

Exercise

Level – 1

1. *Kotwali,* who oversaw the internal affairs and policing of the town, *was an* imperial officer of _______
   - (a) Mughals
   - (b) North India
   - (c) Provinces
   - (d) Mansabdars

2. During the sixteenth and seventeenth centuries the towns consisted of
   1. Artisans
   2. Traders
   3. Administrators
   4. rulers

   Choose the correct answer from the codes given below
   - (a) 1, 2, 3 only
   - (b) 1, 2, 3 and 4
   - (c) 1, 3 and 4 only
   - (d) 2, 3 and 4 only

3. Which of the following cities was not built by the Mughals
   - (a) Agra
   - (b) Delhi
   - (c) Lahore
   - (d) Lucknow

4. In Mughal empire, Mansabdars and jagirdars were used to live in
   - (a) Cities
   - (b) Villages
   - (c) Provinces
   - (d) Emperor palace

5. During the sixteenth and seventeenth centuries the focus of the town was oriented towards
   - (a) the palace
   - (b) the principal mosque
   - (c) the temple.
   - (d) All of the above

6. Find the incorrect pair

European commercial Companies	Bases location
(a) Portuguese	Panaji in 1510
(b) Dutch	Masulipatnam in 1605
(c) British	Surat in 1639
(d) The French	Pondicherry in 1673.

7. British gradually acquired political control after the ______________ that was fought in 1757
   - (a) Battle of Plassey
   - (b) Battle of Panipat
   - (c) Battle of Haldighati
   - (d) None of the above

8. The first all-India census was attempted in _______.
   - (a) 1872
   - (b) 1881
   - (c) 1891
   - (d) 1894

9. By the eighteenth century which of the following became important ports cities?
   - (a) Madras
   - (b) Calcutta
   - (c) Bombay
   - (d) All of the above

Level – 2

10. **Assertion (A):** The English East India Company built its factories and fortified it for protection.

    Reason (R): In Madras, Fort St George, in Calcutta Fort William and in Bombay the Fort marked out the areas of British settlement.
    - (a) Both A and R are true, and R is the correct explanation of A.
    - (b) Both A and R are true, but R is not the correct explanation of A.
    - (c) A is true but R is false.
    - (d) A is false but R is true.

11. Find the incorrect statement with reference to the beginning of modern industrial development in India.
    - (a) Cotton mills were set up by Indian merchants and entrepreneurs in Bombay.
    - (b) European-owned jute mills were established on the outskirts of Calcutta.
    - (c) India never became a modern industrialised country.
    - (d) None of the above

12. Find the true statement with reference to the emergence of new urban settlements after the Revolt of 1857
    - (a) New urban spaces called "Civil Lines" were set up.
    - (b) White people used to live in the Civil Lines.
    - (c) Cantonments were also developed as safe enclaves.
    - (d) All of the above

13. Simla was founded during the course of which of the following events?
    - (a) Gurkha War
    - (b) Anglo-Maratha War
    - (c) Bengal War
    - (d) Gangetic Campaign of the Sikhs

14. In 1864, which of the following viceroys officially moved his council to Simla, setting seal to the practice of shifting capitals during the hot season.
    - (a) Viceroy John Lawrence
    - (b) Lord Willingdon
    - (c) Lord Linlithgow
    - (d) Lord Wavell

15. Find the incorrect statement with reference to the Social life in the new cities

(a) All classes of people were migrating to the big cities.

(b) A new public sphere of debate and discussion emerged.

(c) Social customs, norms and practices came to be questioned.

(d) Another new class within the cities was the poor peasants

16. Consider the following statements

They were Indians who could speak two languages – the local language and English. They worked as agents and merchants, acting as intermediaries between Indian society and the British.

The above statement best describes which of the following categories of people?

(a) Telugu Komatis

(b) Gujarati bankers

(c) Paraiyars and Vanniyars

(d) Dubashes

17. Vellalars were the rural caste people of which of the following regions?

(a) Madras   (b) Andhra Pradesh

(c) Kerala   (d) Pondicherry

18. Calcutta had grown from which of the following villages

1. Sutanati   2. Kolkata

3. Govindapur.   4. Maidan

Choose the correct answer from the codes given below

(a) 1, 2, 3 only

(b) 1, 2, 3 and 4

(c) 1, 3 and 4 only

(d) 2, 3 and 4 only

19. Which of the following were the architectural style of Bombay

(a) Neo-classical or the new classical

(b) Neo-Gothic

(c) Indo-Saracenic

(d) All of the above

20. In 1757, the Nawab of Bengal ______________ was defeated in the Battle of Plassey by the East India Company

(a) Azim-us-Shan

(b) Shah Alam II.

(c) Sirajudaula

(d) Ala-ud-Din Haidar Jung

Answers

Level-1

1. (a)   2. (b)   3. (d)   4. (a)   5. (d)   6. (c)   7. (a)   8. (a)   9. (d)

Level-2

10. (a)   11. (d)   12. (d)   13. (a)   14. (a)   15. (d)   16. (d)   17. (a)   18. (a)   19. (d)

20. (c)

Explanations

Level – 1

1. a • The imperial officer of North India – *kotwali ,* who oversaw the internal affairs and policing of the town.

2. b • Towns were peopled with artisans, traders, administrators and rulers.

3. d • During the sixteenth and seventeenth centuries the towns built by the Mughals like Agra, Delhi and Lahore were important centres of imperial administration and control.

4. a • *Mansabdars* and *jagirdars* who were assigned territories in different parts of the empire usually maintained houses in these cities

5. d • The focus of the town was oriented towards the palace and the principal mosque.

• In the towns of South India such as Madurai and Kanchipuram the principal focus was the temple.

6. c • The European commercial Companies had set up base in different places early during the Mughal era: the Portuguese in Panaji in 1510, the Dutch in Masulipatnam in 1605, the British in Madras in 1639 and the French in Pondicherry in1673.

7. a • The British gradually acquired political control after the Battle of Plassey in 1757, and the trade of the English East India Company expanded

8. a • By the mid-nineteenth century several local censuses had been carried out in different regions. The first all-India census was attempted in 1872.

• Thereafter, from 1881, decennial (conducted every ten years) censuses became a regular feature.

9. d • By the eighteenth century Madras, Calcutta and Bombay had become important ports.

• The settlements that came up here were convenient points for collecting goods.

Level – 2

10. a • The English East India Company built its factories and fortified it for protection.

• In Madras, Fort St George, in Calcutta Fort William and in Bombay the Fort marked out the areas of British settlement.

11. d • After the 1850s, cotton mills were set up by Indian merchants and entrepreneurs in Bombay, and European-owned jute mills were established on the outskirts of Calcutta.

• This was the beginning of modern industrial development in India.

• India never became a modern industrialised country, since discriminatory colonial policies limited the levels of industrial development.

12. d • New urban spaces (Safe enclaves) called "Civil Lines" were set up.

• White people began to live in the Civil Lines.

• Cantonments– places where Indian troops under European command were stationed – were also developed as safe enclaves.

13. a • Simla was founded during the course of the Gurkha War (1815-16); the Anglo-Maratha War of 1818 led to British interest in Mount Abu; and Darjeeling was wrested from the rulers of Sikkim in 1835.

14. a • In 1864 the Viceroy John Lawrence officially moved his council to Simla, setting seal to the practice of shifting capitals during the hot season.

15. d • Within the cities new social groups were formed and the old identities of people were no longer important.

• All classes of people were migrating to the big cities.

• A new public sphere of debate and discussion emerged.

• Social customs, norms and practices came to be questioned.

• Another new class within the cities was the labouring poor or the working class.

16. d • The *dubashes* were Indians who could speak two languages – the local language and English.

• They worked as agents and merchants, acting as intermediaries between Indian society and the British.

17. a

18. a • Calcutta had grown from three villages called Sutanati, Kolkata and Govindapur.

19. d • As Bombay's economy grew, many new buildings were constructed at this time.

 • The architectural style was usually European.

 • Initially, these buildings were at odds with the traditional Indian buildings.

 • Gradually, Indians too got used to European architecture and made it their own

20. c • In 1756, Sirajudaula, the Nawab of Bengal, attacked Calcutta and sacked the small fort which the British traders had built as their depot for goods.

 • Subsequently, in 1757, when Sirajudaula was defeated in the Battle of Plassey, the East India Company decided to build a new fort, one that could not be easily attacked.

CHAPTER 13

THEME THIRTEEN

Mahatma Gandhi and the Nationalist Movement

Civil Disobedience and Beyond

1. A Leader Announces Himself

- In January 1915, Mohandas Karamchand Gandhi returned to his homeland after two decades of residence abroad.

Condition when Gandhi arrived India

- The India that Mahatma Gandhi came back to in 1915 was rather different from the one that he had left in 1893.
- The Indian National Congress now had branches in most major cities and towns. Through the Swadeshi movement of 1905-07 it had greatly broadened its appeal among the middle classes.
- That movement had thrown up some towering leaders – among them Bal Gangadhar Tilak of Maharashtra, Bipin Chandra Pal of Bengal, and Lala Lajpat Rai of Punjab. The three were known as "Lal, Bal and Pal".
- There was a group of "Moderates" who preferred a more gradual and persuasive approach. Among these Moderates was Gandhiji's acknowledged political mentor, Gopal Krishna Gokhale, as well as Mohammad Ali Jinnah, who, like Gandhiji, was a lawyer of Gujarati extraction trained in London.

After Arrival

- On Gokhale's advice, Gandhiji spent a year travelling around British India, getting to know the land
- His first major public appearance was at the opening of the Banaras Hindu University (BHU) in February 1916.
- He had been invited on account of his work in South Africa, rather than his status within India.

- At the annual Congress, held in Lucknow in December 1916, he was approached by a peasant from Champaran in Bihar, who told him about the harsh treatment of peasants by British indigo planters.

2. The Making and Unmaking of Non-cooperation

- Mahatma Gandhi was to spend much of 1917 in Champaran, seeking to obtain for the peasants security of tenure as well as the freedom to cultivate the crops of their choice. The following year, 1918, Gandhiji was involved in two campaigns in his home state of Gujarat.
- First, he intervened in a labour dispute in Ahmedabad, demanding better working conditions for the textile mill workers. Then he joined peasants in Kheda in asking the state for the remission of taxes following the failure of their harvest.
- During the Great War of 1914-18, the British had instituted censorship of the press and permitted detention without trial. Now, on the recommendation of a committee chaired by Sir Sidney Rowlatt, these tough measures were continued. In response, Gandhiji called for a countrywide campaign against the "Rowlatt Act".
- Gandhiji was detained while proceeding to Punjab, even as prominent local Congressmen were arrested.
- The situation in the province grew progressively tenser, reaching a bloody climax in Amritsar in April 1919, when a British Brigadier ordered his troops to open fire on a nationalist meeting - known as the Jallianwala Bagh massacre.

- Emboldened by the success of Rowlatt Syagrah, Gandhiji called for a campaign of "non-cooperation" with British rule. Indians who wished colonialism to end were asked to stop attending schools, colleges and law courts, and not pay taxes.

- To further broaden the struggle he had joined hands with the Khilafat Movement that sought to restore the Caliphate, a symbol of Pan-Islamism

Knitting a popular movement

- Non-cooperation was negative enough to be peaceful but positive enough to be effective.

- Peasants, workers, and others interpreted and acted upon the call to "non-cooperate" with colonial rule in ways that best suited their interests, rather than conform to the dictates laid down from above.

- As a consequence of the Non-Cooperation Movement the British Raj was shaken to its foundations for the first time since the Revolt of 1857.

A people's leader

- While other nationalist leaders dressed formally, wearing a Western suit or an Indian *bandgala*, Gandhiji went among the people in a simple *dhoti* or loincloth.

- Meanwhile, he spent part of each day working on the *charkha* (spinning wheel), and encouraged other nationalists to do likewise.

- The act of spinning allowed Gandhiji to break the boundaries that prevailed within the traditional caste system, between mental labour and manual labour.

- New branches of the Congress were set up in various parts of India.

- A series of "Praja Mandals" were established to promote the nationalist creed in the princely states. Gandhiji encouraged the communication of the nationalist message in the mother tongue.

- Between 1917 and 1922, a group of highly talented Indians attached themselves to Gandhiji. They included Mahadev Desai, Vallabh Bhai Patel, J.B. Kripalani, Subhas Chandra Bose, Abul Kalam Azad, Jawaharlal Nehru, Sarojini Naidu, Govind Ballabh Pant and C. Rajagopalachari.

- He vouched for removal of untouchability and promotion of Hindu Muslim unity

3. The Salt Satyagraha A Case Study

- In 1928, there was an all-India campaign in opposition to the all-White Simon Commission, sent from England to enquire into conditions in the colony. Gandhiji did not himself participate in this movement, although he gave it his blessings, as he also did to a peasant satyagraha in Bardoli in the same year.

- In the end of December 1929, the Congress held its annual session in the city of Lahore.

- The meeting was significant for two things: the election of Jawaharlal Nehru as President, signifying the passing of the baton of leadership to the younger generation; and the proclamation of commitment to "Purna Swaraj", or complete independence.

- On 26 January 1930, "Independence Day" was observed, with the national flag being hoisted in different venues, and patriotic songs being sung

Dandi

- The state monopoly over salt was deeply unpopular; by making it his target, Gandhiji hoped to mobilise a wider discontent against British rule.

- Viceroy Lord Irwin, Irwin failed to grasp the significance of the action.

- On 12 March 1930, Gandhiji began walking from his ashram at Sabarmati towards the ocean. He reached his destination three weeks later, making a fistful of salt as he did and thereby making himself a criminal in the eyes of the law.

Dialogues

- Salt March which forced upon the British the realisation that their Raj would not last forever.

- To that end, the British government convened a series of "Round Table Conferences" in London. The first meeting was held in November 1930, but without the pre-eminent political leader in India, thus rendering it an exercise in futility.

- "Gandhi-Irwin Pact', by the terms of which civil disobedience would be called off, all prisoners released, and salt manufacture allowed along the coast.

- A second Round Table Conference was held in London in the latter part of 1931. Here, Gandhiji represented the Congress. However, his claims that his party represented all of India came under challenge from the Muslim League, the Prince and BR Ambedkar.

- After the second round table conference, Gandhiji returned to India and resumed civil disobedience.

- In 1935, however, a new Government of India Act promised some form of representative government. Two years later, in an election held on the basis of a restricted franchise, the Congress won a comprehensive victory.

- In September 1939, two years after the Congress ministries assumed office, the Second World War broke out. Congress promised Congress support to the war effort if the British, in return, promised to grant India independence once hostilities ended.

- The offer was refused. In protest, the Congress ministries resigned in October 1939.

- In the spring of 1942, Churchill was persuaded to send one of his ministers, Sir Stafford Cripps, to India to try and forge a compromise with Gandhiji and the Congress. Talks broke down, however, after the Congress insisted tha**t if it was to help the British defend India from the Axis powers, then the Viceroy had first to appoint an Indian as the Defence Member of his Executive Council.**

4. Quit India

- After the failure of the Cripps Mission, Mahatma Gandhi decided to launch his third major movement against British rule. This was the "Quit India" campaign, which began in August 1942.

- Particularly active in the underground resistance were socialist members of the Congress, such as Jayaprakash Narayan.

- In several districts, such as Satara in the west and Medinipur in the east, "independent" governments were proclaimed.

- Early in 1946 fresh elections were held to the provincial legislatures. The Congress swept the "General" category, but in the seats specifically reserved for Muslims the League won an overwhelming majority.

- A Cabinet Mission sent in the summer of 1946 failed to get the Congress and the League to agree on a federal system that would keep India together while allowing the provinces a degree of autonomy.

- After the talks broke down, Jinnah called for a "Direct Action Day" to press the League's demand for Pakistan. On the designated day, 16 August 1946, bloody riots broke out in Calcutta.

- The violence spread to rural Bengal, then to Bihar, and then across the country to the United Provinces and the Punjab.

- In February 1947, Wavell was replaced as Viceroy by Lord Mountbatten.

- The formal transfer of power was fixed for 15 August. When that day came, it was celebrated with gusto in different parts of India.

5. The Last Heroic Days

Gandhiji marked the day with a 24-hour fast. The freedom he had struggled so long for had come at an unacceptable price, with a nation divided and Hindus and Muslims at each other's.

Exercise

Level – 1

1. The claims of single party representation for the entire India by Gandhi at the Second Round table conference was rejected by who among the following?

(a) The Muslim League

(b) The Princely States

(c) BR Ambedkar

(d) All of the above

2. Which of the following provisions were agreed upon by the Gandhi Irwin Pact?

(a) Calling off of the civil disobedience

(b) Salt manufacture allowed along the coast.

(c) Both (a) and (b)

(d) Release of all prisoners

3. Who among the following leaders did no associate themselves with the Gandhian style of politics ?

(a) Subhas Chandra Bose

(b) Govind Ballabh Pant

(c) J.B. Kripalani

(d) None of the above

4. The Praja Mandals were established to promote the nationalist creed in which of the following parts of the pre-independent India?

(a) The southern states

(b) Jammu and Kashmir

(c) Bihar and Bengal

(d) The pricely states

5. The Civil Disobedience Movement was resumed by which of the following event ?

(a) The First Rounf Table Conference

(b) The Second Rounf Table Conference

(c) The Third Rounf Table Conference

(d) None of the above

6. Identify the incorrect statement with respect to the Round Table Conferences ?

(a) All the conferences were convened by the British Government in London.

(b) The first meeting was held in November 1930,

(c) There was no pre-eminent political leader in India in the First Round Table Conference

(d) None of the above

7. The people were asked to contribute to the Non-cooperation Movement through which of the following processes?

(a) To stop attending schools

(b) Not resorting to law courts

(c) Not paying the taxes

(d) All of the above

8. Gandhiji spent a year travelling around British India, getting to know the land, on the advice of who among the following leaders?

(a) J.B. Kripalani

(b) Abul Kalam Azad

(c) Govind Ballabh Pant

(d) Gopal Krishna Gokhale

9. Gandhiji joined hands with the Khilafat Movement to further broaden the struggle under which of the following movement?

(a) Swadeshi and Boycott Movement

(b) Rowlatt Satyagrah

(c) Non Cooperation Movement

(d) None of the above

10. Identify the correct statements:

(a) Both Gokhale and Mohammad jinnah belonged to the group of Moderates.

(b) Both Gandhi and Jinnah were lawyers by profession who were trained in London.

(c) Both (a) and (b)

(d) None of the above

Level – 2

11. Consider the following incidents

1. A Cabinet Mission was sent to get the Congress and the League to agree on a federal system

2. Jinnah called for a "Direct Action Day"

3. Sir Stafford Cripps visited India

Which of the following is the correct chronological order from earliest to latest

(a) 1-2-3

(b) 3-1-2

(c) 1-3-2

(d) 2-1-3

12. Which of the following is not the correct statement with difference to the Indian national Congress?

(a) A resolution was passed on "the rights of minorities" at the inititive of Gandhi and Nehru

(b) The party had never accepted the "two-nation theory".

(c) The Congress wished to "assure the minorities in India that it will continue to protect

(d) The party, for the sake of peace, accepted the rightfulness of state religion

13. Which of the following statements is incorrect with reference to the elections of 1946?

(a) The elections were held in the provincial legislatures.

(b) Congress swept the "General" category.

(c) The performance of the Muslim League assured its diminishing importance even among the Muslims.

(d) There was the provision for a separate electorate in the election

14. Which of the following incidents is/are related to the quit India movement?

(a) Independent governments at Satara in the west and Medinipur in the east.

(b) Underground resistance by socialist members of the Congress, such as Jayaprakash Narayan.

(c) Observation of "Independence Day" throughout the country.

(d) Both (a) and (b)

15. The talks that were initiated in 1942 by Sir Stafford Cripps, broke down on which of the following grounds?

(a) Viceroy had first to appoint an Indian as the Defence Member

(b) Immediate transfer of power

(c) Release of the prisoners of the Indian National Army

(d) Release of the leaders.

16. He was the Viceroy of India during the Dandi March carried by Gandhi. He is known for having made a declaration that Britain would be committed to the eventual dominion status of India. The above description is related to who among the following?

(a) Lord Linlithgow   (b) Lord Wavell

(c) Lord Mountbatten   (d) Lord Irwin

17. The session of the Indian National Congress was significant for two things: the election of Jawaharlal Nehru as President, signifying the passing of the baton of leadership to the younger generation; and the proclamation of commitment to "Purna Swaraj", or complete independence. The session was held in which year?

(a) 1926   (b) 1929

(c) 1930   (d) 1936

18. During the course of Indian Freedom struggle, a group of peasants attacked and torched a police station in the hamlet of Chauri Chaura, in the United Provinces (now, Uttar Pradesh and Uttaranchal). Several constables perished in the conflagration. As a response to this, which of the following movements was called off?

(a) Rowlatt Satyagrah

(b) Quit India Movement

(c) Non Cooperation Movement

(d) Civil Disoedience Movement

19. After the return form South Africa, the first major public appearance was at the opening of which of the following Universities?

(a) Patna University

(b) Banaras Hindu University

(c) Madras Colleege

(d) College of Engineering, Pune

20. Which of the following events had already happened before the return of Gandhi from South Africa?

(a) Expansion of the the Indian National Congress in most major cities and towns.

(b) Swadeshi movement broadened its appeal among the middle classes.

(c) Emergence of leaders like Lala Lajpat Rai of Punjab.

(d) All of the above

21. Which of the following incidents led to the censorship of the press and permission to detention without trial in India for the first time?

(a) Formation of the Indian National Army

(b) The Great War of 1914-18

(c) The recommendation of the committee chaired by Sir Sidney Rowlatt

(d) None of the above

Answers

Level-1

1. (d)   **2.** (c)   **3.** (d)   **4.** (d)   **5.** (b)   **6.** (d)   **7.** (d)   **8.** (d)   **9.** (c)   **10.** (c)

Level-2

11. (b)   **12.** (d)   **13.** (c)   **14.** (d)   **15.** (a)   **16.** (d)   **17.** (b)   **18.** (c)   **19.** (b)   **20.** (d)

21. (b)

Explanations

Level – 1

1. d A second Round Table Conference was held in London in the latter part of 1931. Here, Gandhiji represented the Congress. However, his claims that his party represented all of India came under challenge from the Muslim League, the Prince and BR Ambedkar.

After the second round table conference, Gandhiji returned to India and resumed civil disobedience.

2. c "Gandhi-Irwin Pact', by the terms of which civil disobedience would be called off, all prisoners released, and salt manufacture allowed along the coast.

3. d Between 1917 and 1922, a group of highly talented Indians attached themselves to Gandhiji. They included Mahadev Desai, Vallabh Bhai Patel, J.B. Kripalani, Subhas Chandra Bose, Abul Kalam Azad, Jawaharlal Nehru, Sarojini Naidu, Govind Ballabh Pant and C. Rajagopalachari.

4. d A series of "Praja Mandals" were established to promote the nationalist creed in the princely states. Gandhiji encouraged the communication of the nationalist message in the mother tongue.

5. b After the second round table conference, Gandhiji returned to India and resumed civil disobedience.

6. d All the statements are correct. The British government convened a series of "Round Table Conferences" in London. The first meeting was held in November 1930, but without the pre-eminent political leader in India, thus rendering it an exercise in futility

7. d Emboldened by its success, Gandhiji called for a campaign of "non-cooperation" with British rule. Indians who wished colonialism to end were asked to stop attending schools, colleges and law courts, and not pay taxes.

8. d On Gokhale's advice, Gandhiji spent a year travelling around British India, getting to know the land

9. c To further broaden the struggle under the Non Cooperation Movement he had joined hands with the Khilafat Movement that sought to restore the Caliphate, a symbol of Pan-Islamism

10. c There was a group of "Moderates" who preferred a more gradual and persuasive approach. Among these Moderates was Gandhiji's acknowledged political mentor, Gopal Krishna Gokhale, as well as Mohammad Ali Jinnah, who, like Gandhiji, was a lawyer of Gujarati extraction trained in London.

Level – 2

11. b In the spring of 1942, Churchill was persuaded to send one of his ministers, Sir Stafford Cripps, to India to try and forge a compromise with Gandhiji and the Congress.

A Cabinet Mission sent in the summer of 1946 failed to get the Congress and the League to agree on a federal system that would keep India together while allowing the provinces a degree of autonomy.

After the talks broke down, Jinnah called for a "Direct Action Day" to press the League's demand for Pakistan. On the designated day, 16 August 1946, bloody riots broke out in Calcutta.

12. d At the initiative of Gandhiji and Nehru, the Congress now passed a resolution on "the rights of minorities". The party had never accepted the "two-nation theory": forced against its will to accept Partition, it still believed that "India is a land of many religions and many races, and must remain so". Whatever be the situation in Pakistan, India would be "a democratic secular State where all citizens enjoy full rights and are equally entitled to the protection of the State, irrespective of the religion to which they belong". The Congress wished to "assure the minorities in India that it will continue to protect, to the best of its ability, their citizen rights against aggression".

13. c In the seats specifically reserved for Muslims, the Muslim League won an overwhelming majority.

14. d Particularly active in the underground resistance during Qui India movement were socialist members of the Congress, such as Jayaprakash Narayan. In several districts, such as Satara in the west and Medinipur in the east, "independent" governments were proclaimed.

On 26 January 1930, "Independence Day" was observed, with the national flag being hoisted in different venues, and patriotic songs being sung

15. a In the spring of 1942, Churchill was persuaded to send one of his ministers, Sir Stafford Cripps, to India to try and forge a compromise with Gandhiji and the Congress. Talks broke down, however, after the Congress insisted that if it was to help the British defend India from the Axis powers, then the Viceroy had first to appoint an Indian as the Defence Member of his Executive Council.

16. d Lord Irwin was the Viceroy of India during the Dandi March carried by Gandhi. Viceroy Lord Irwin, Irwin failed to grasp the significance of the action.

17. b In the end of December 1929, the Congress held its annual session in the city of Lahore. The meeting was significant for two things: the election of Jawaharlal Nehru as President, signifying the passing of the baton of leadership to the younger generation; and the proclamation of commitment to "Purna Swaraj", or complete independence.

18. c In February 1922, a group of peasants attacked and torched a police station in the hamlet of Chauri Chaura, in the United Provinces (now, Uttar Pradesh and Uttaranchal). Several constables perished in the conflagration. On this, Gabdhi called off the NCM.

19. b His first major public appearance was at the opening of the Banaras Hindu University (BHU) in February 1916.

20. d The India that Mahatma Gandhi came back to in 1915 was rather different from the one that he had left in 1893. The Indian National Congress now had branches in most major cities and towns. Through the Swadeshi movement of 1905-07 it had greatly broadened its appeal among the middle classes.

That movement had thrown up some towering leaders – among them Bal Gangadhar Tilak of Maharashtra, Bipin Chandra Pal of Bengal, and Lala Lajpat Rai of Punjab. The three were known as "Lal, Bal and Pal"

21. b During the Great War of 1914-18, the British had instituted censorship of the press and permitted detention without trial. The committee chaired by Sir Sidney Rowlatt recommended only its continuation.

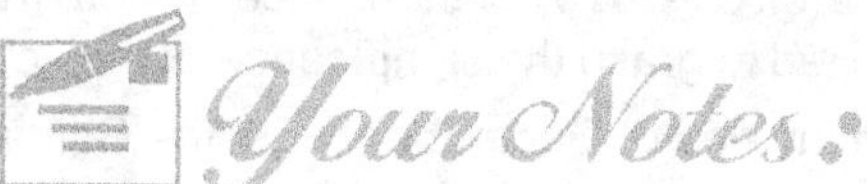
Your Notes :

CHAPTER 14

Understanding Partition

- The Partition of British India into the sovereign states of India and Pakistan (with its western and eastern wings) led to many sudden developments.

1. A Momentous Marker

- The boundaries between the two new states were not officially known until two days *after* formal independence.
- Partition generated memories, hatreds, stereotypes and identities that still continue to shape the history of people on both sides of the border.

2. Why and How Did Partition Happen?

- Scholars suggest that separate electorates for Muslims, created by the colonial government in 1909 and expanded in 1919, crucially shaped the nature of communal politics.
- Separate electorates created a temptation for politicians working within this system to use sectarian slogans and gather a following by distributing favours to their own religious groups.
- Communal identities were consolidated by a host of other developments in the early twentieth century. Muslims were angered by "music-before-mosque", by the cow protection movement, and by the efforts of the Arya Samaj to bring back to the Hindu fold (*shuddhi*) those who had recently converted to Islam.
- Hinds were angered by the rapid spread of *tabligh* (propaganda) and *tanzim* (organisation) after 1923.

What is Communalism?

- Communalism refers to a politics that seeks to unify one community around a religious identity in hostile opposition to another community. It seeks to define this community identity as fundamental and fixed. It attempts to consolidate this identity and present it as natural – as if people were born into the identity, as if the identities do not evolve through history over time.
- In order to unify the community, communalism suppresses distinctions within the community and emphasises the essential unity of the community against other communities.
- Communalism, then, is a particular kind of politicisation of religious identity, an ideology that seeks to promote conflict between religious communities.

The Lucknow Pact

- The Lucknow Pact of December 1916 was an understanding between the Congress and the Muslim League (controlled by the UP-based "Young Party") whereby the Congress accepted separate electorates. The pact provided a joint political platform for the Moderates, Radicals and the Muslim League

Arya Samaj

- A North Indian Hindu reform organisation of the late nineteenth and early twentieth centuries, particularly active in the Punjab, which sought to revive Vedic learning and combine it with modern education in the sciences.

The Muslim League

- Initially floated in Dhaka in 1906, the Muslim League was quickly taken over by the U.P.-based Muslim elite. The party began to make demands for autonomy for the Muslim-majority areas of the subcontinent and/or Pakistan in the 1940s.

Hindu Mahasabha

- Founded in 1915, the Hindu Mahasabha was a Hindu party that remained confined to North India. It aimed to unite Hindu society by encouraging the Hindus to transcend the divisions of caste and sect. It sought to define Hindu identity in opposition to Muslim identity.

The provincial elections of 1937 and the Congress ministries

- In 1937, elections to the provincial legislatures were held for the first time.

- Only about 10 to 12 per cent of the population enjoyed the right to vote.

- The Congress did well in the elections, winning an absolute majority in five out of eleven provinces and forming governments in seven of them. It did badly in the constituencies reserved for Muslims, but the Muslim League also fared poorly

- The League failed to win a single seat in the North West Frontier Province (NWFP) and could capture only two out of 84 reserved constituencies in the Punjab and three out of 33 in Sind.

- In the United Provinces, the Muslim League wanted to form a joint government with the Congress. The Congress had won an absolute majority in the province, so it rejected the offer. Some scholars argue that this rejection convinced the League for a separate nation for Muslims.

- But Jinnah's insistence that the League be recognised as the "sole spokesman" of Muslims could convince few at the time. Though popular in the United Provinces, Bombay and Madras, social support for the League was still fairly weak in three of the provinces from which Pakistan was to be carved out just ten years later – Bengal, the NWFP and the Punjab.

- The Congress ministries also contributed to the widening rift. In the United Provinces, the party had rejected the Muslim League proposal for a coalition government partly because the League tended to support landlordism, which the Congress wished to abolish, although the party had not yet taken any concrete steps in that direction.

- Nor did the Congress achieve any substantial gains in the "Muslim mass contact" programme it launched.

- Maulana Azad, an important Congress leader, pointed out in 1937 that members of the Congress were not allowed to join the League

- Only in December 1938 did the Congress Working Committee declare that Congress members could not be members of the Mahasabha.

The "Pakistan" Resolution

- On 23 March 1940, the League moved a resolution demanding a measure of autonomy for the Muslim-majority areas of the subcontinent. This ambiguous resolution never mentioned partition or Pakistan

- Sikandar Hayat Khan, Punjab Premier and leader of the Unionist Party, who had drafted the resolution, declared in a Punjab assembly speech on 1 March 1941 that he was opposed to a Pakistan that would mean "Muslim Raj here and Hindu Raj elsewhere

- He reiterated his plea for a loose (united), confederation with considerable autonomy for the confederating units.

- The origins of the Pakistan demand have also been traced back to the Urdu poet Mohammad Iqbal, the writer of *"Sare Jahan Se Achha Hindustan Hamara"*. However he only visualized reorganisation of Muslim-majority areas in north-western India into an autonomous unit within a single, loosely structured Indian federation.

Post-War developments

- When negotiations were begun again in 1945, the British agreed to create an entirely Indian central Executive Council, except for the Viceroy and the Commander-in-Chief of the armed forces, as a preliminary step towards full independence.

- Provincial elections were again held in 1946. The Congress swept the general constituencies, capturing 91.3 per cent of the non-Muslim vote. The League's success in the seats reserved for Muslims was equally spectacular: it won all 30 reserved constituencies in the Centre with 86.6 per cent of the Muslim vote and 442 out of 509 seats in the provinces.

- **However,** franchise was extremely limited. About 10 to 12 per cent of the population enjoyed the right to vote in the provincial elections and a mere one per cent in the elections for the Central Assembly.

A possible alternative to Partition

- In March 1946 the British Cabinet sent a three-member mission to Delhi to examine the League's demand

- Recommendation by the Cabinet Mission: India was to remain united. It was to have a weak central government controlling only foreign affairs, defence and communications with the existing provincial assemblies being grouped into three sections while electing the constituent assembly: Section A for the Hindu-majority provinces, and Sections B and C for the Muslim-majority provinces of the north-west and the north-east (including Assam) respectively.

- They would have the power to set up intermediate-level executives and legislatures of their own

- Initially all the major parties accepted this plan. But the agreement was short-lived because it was based on mutually opposed interpretations of the plan.

- **Initially all the major parties accepted this plan. But the agreement was short-lived because it was based on mutually opposed interpretations of the plan.**

- Ultimately, therefore, neither the League nor the Congress agreed to the Cabinet Mission's proposal.

- This made the idea of partition even more inevitable. Only Mahatma Gandhi and Khan Abdul Ghaffar Khan of the NWFP continued to firmly oppose the idea of partition.

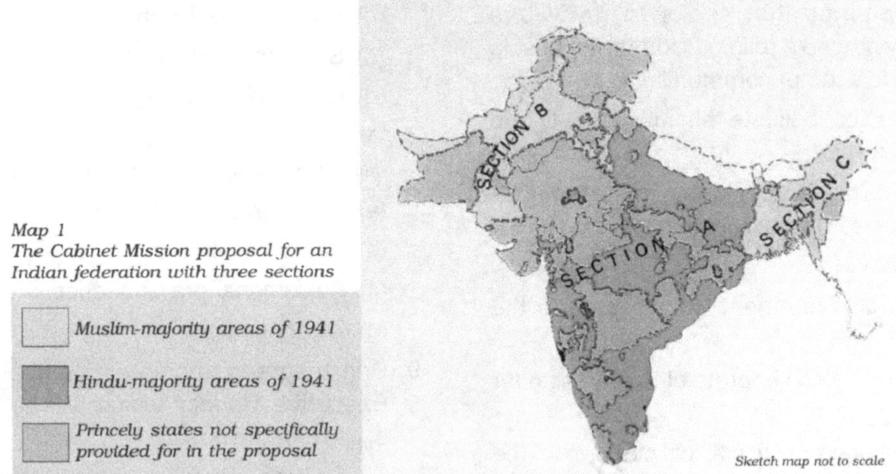

Map 1
The Cabinet Mission proposal for an
Indian federation with three sections

Muslim-majority areas of 1941

Hindu-majority areas of 1941

Princely states not specifically
provided for in the proposal

Sketch map not to scale

Towards Partition

- After withdrawing its support to the Cabinet Mission plan, the Muslim League decided on "Direct Action" for winning its Pakistan demand. It announced 16 August 1946 as "Direct Action Day".

- It was in March 1947 that the Congress high command voted for dividing the Punjab into two halves, one with Muslim majority and the other with Hindu/Sikh majority; and it asked for the application of a similar principle to Bengal.

Exercise

Level – 1

1. Which of the following statements correctly represent the idea of communalism?

(a) It is the politics that seeks to unify one community around a religious identity in hostile opposition to another community.

(b) It attempts to consolidate religious identity and present it as natural

(c) It suppresses distinctions within the community and emphasises the essential unity.

(d) All of the above

2. Find the incorrect statement with respect to the Lucknow pact:

(a) Congress accepted separate electorates under the pact.

(b) The pact provided a joint political platform for the Moderates, the Muslim League but not the radicals.

(c) Both (a) and (b)

(d) None of the above

3. The terms tabligh and tanzim refer to which of the following ?

(a) Religious pilgrimage paid by the particular community

(b) Propaganda and organization

(c) Forms of offering prayers

(d) Institutions for religious ceremonies

4. The elections to the provincial legislatures were held for the first time in __

(a) 1919　　　　　　(b) 1925

(c) 1937　　　　　　(d) 1946

5. Which of the following are the provinces from which the new country of Pakistan was decided to be carved out at the time of Independence?

(a) The NWFP　　　　(b) Punjab

(c) Bengal　　　　　(d) All of the above

6. The "Muslim mass contact" was launched by which of the following organizations?

(a) The Indian National Congress

(b) The Muslim League

(c) The Ahmadiya Movement followers

(d) None of the above

7. The resolution of the Muslim League passed in March 1940 was drafted by who among the following?

(a) Nawab Khwaja Salimullah

(b) Hakin Azmal Khan

(c) Sikandar Hayat Khan

(d) None of the above

8. Who among the following was the writer of "Sare Jahan Se Achha Hindustan Hamara?

(a) Mohammad Iqbal

(d) Rabindranath Tagore

(c) Bankimchandra Chatterjee

(d) Zafar Ali Khan

9. British agreed to create an entirely Indian central Executive Council which will be entirely Indian, except for the post of

(a) Commander-in-Chief of the armed forces

(b) Viceroy

(c) Both (a) and (b)

(d) Only (a)

10. Which of the following led to the breakdown of talks for the transfer of power under the Cabinet Mission?

(a) Different interpretations

(b) Reluctance and violence by communal groups

(c) The demand of the League to choose all Muslim members of the executive council

(d) None of the above

Level – 2

11. Which of the following statements is incorrect with reference to the Arya Samaj?

(a) It was North Indian Hindu reform organisation.

(b) It sought to revive Vedic learning.

(c) It denied the acceptance and validity of modern education in the sciences.

(d) None of the above

12. Which of the following is the reason that contributed to communalism in the colonial India?

(a) Separate electorates created by the colonial government in 1919.

(b) Suddhi efforts by the members of the Arya Samaj

(c) Cow Protection Movements

(d) Both (b) and (c)

13. Which of the following statement is correct with reference to the elections that were held in 1937?

   (a) Less than 20% of the population had the right to vote.

   (b) Congress did well with an absolute majority in all the provinces it had contested for.

   (c) The Muslim league could do well only in the constituency reserved for Muslims.

   (d) The congress good porn party in all the 11 provinces.

14. After the 1937 elections, Congress rejected the proposal of Muslim league to form a coalition government in the United Provinces. The rejection was due to which of the following reasons?

   (a) Communal tensions

   (b) British intervention

   (c) League's support for Landlordism

   (d) Congress support for linguistic preferences.

15. Which of the following statements is correct?

   (a) The members of Congress were asked not to join the Muslim league from 1935 onwards.

   (b) The members of Congress were asked to not join the Maha Sabha from 1936 onwards.

   (c) Both (a) and (b)

   (d) None of the above

16. Which of the following statements is correct with reference to the demand for a separate Pakistan?

   (a) On 23 March 1940, a resolution demanded a measure of autonomy for the Muslim- majority areas by the Muslim League.

   (b) The 1940 resolution passed by the Muslim league clearly mentioned partition and Pakistan for the first time.

   (c) Only (a)

   (d) Both (a) and (b)

17. Consider the image

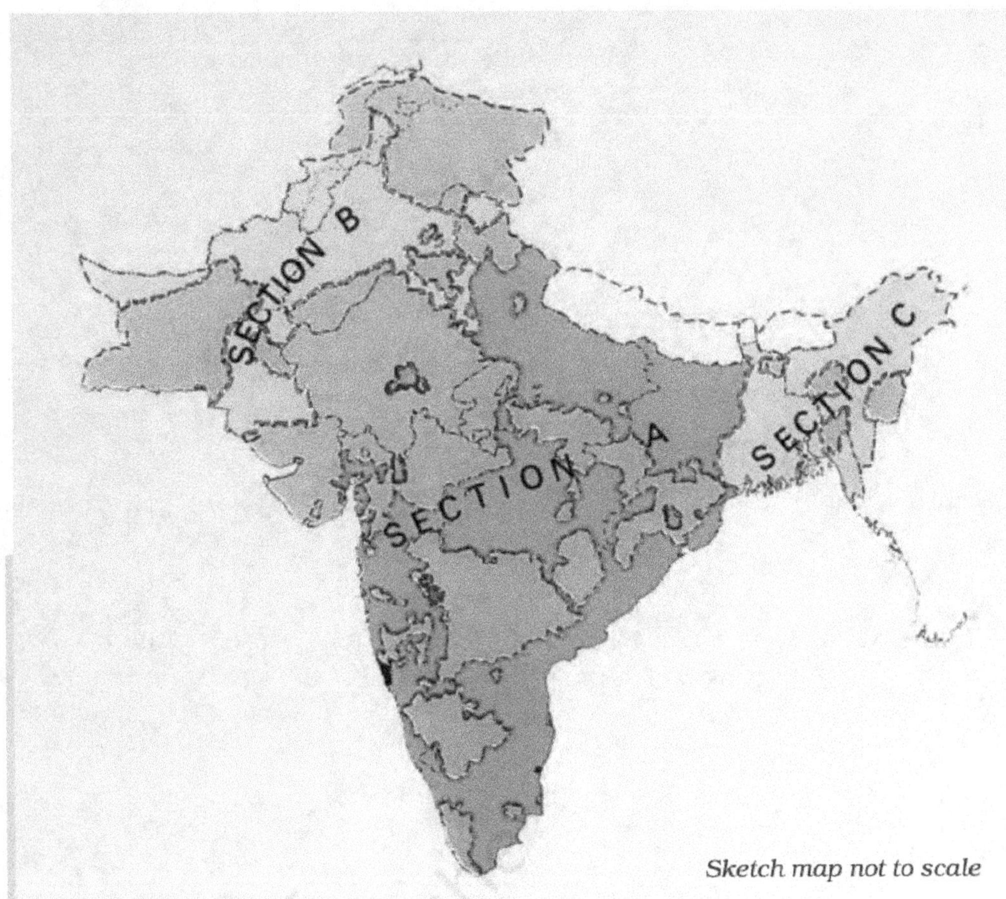

Sketch map not to scale

The division of provinces in the above image was proposed by which of the following committees/missions?

(a) The Cripps Mission

(b) The August offer

(c) The Cabinet Mission

(d) The Hunter Commission

18. Which of the following is not correct with reference to the performance of different parties in the provincial elections held in 1946?

(a) Congress swept more than 90% of non-Muslim votes in general constituencies.

(b) The Muslim League won all the reserved constituencies in the centre.

(c) More than 80% of the Muslim population in the country voted for the Muslim league.

(d) For the first time, the Muslim League established itself as a dominant national party.

19. Which of the following statement is correct with reference to the Cabinet Mission?

(a) Initially all the major parties accepted this plan.

(b) Different parties interpreted the plan proposed by the mission differently.

(c) It recommended that India should go for partition in order to avoid further damage.

(d) Only (a) and (b)

20. Which of the following statements is correct with reference to the performance of the Muslim League in elections.

(a) The 1936 provincial elections were the first such election where the Muslim league proved itself as dominant.

(b) The first time the Muslim league could get a massive victory was in the North-West Frontier province.

(c) Both (a) and (b)

(d) None of the above

Answers

Level-1

1. (d)	**2.** (b)	**3.** (b)	**4.** (c)	**5.** (d)	**6.** (b)	**7.** (c)	**8.** (a)	**9.** (c)	**10.** (c)

Level-2

11. (c)	**12.** (d)	**13.** (a)	**14.** (c)	**15.** (d)	**16.** (c)	**17.** (c)	**18.** (c)	**19.** (d)	**20.** (d)

Explanations

Level – 1

1. d Communalism refers to a politics that seeks to unify one community around a religious identity in hostile opposition to another community. It seeks to define this community identity as fundamental and fixed. It attempts to consolidate this identity and present it as natural – as if people were born into the identity, as if the identities do not evolve through history over time.

In order to unify the community, communalism suppresses distinctions within the community and emphasises the essential unity of the community against other communities.

Communalism, then, is a particular kind of politicisation of religious identity, an ideology that seeks to promote conflict between religious communities.

2. b The Lucknow Pact

The Lucknow Pact of December 1916 was an understanding between the Congress and the Muslim League (controlled by the UP-based "Young Party") whereby the Congress accepted separate electorates. **The pact provided a joint political platform for the Moderates, Radicals and the Muslim League**

3. b There were many reasons that aggravated the Muslims and indus and pushed them further towards communal extremes. Hindus were angered by the rapid spread of *tabligh* (propaganda) and *tanzim* (organisation) after 1923.

4. c In 1937, elections to the provincial legislatures were held for the first time

5. d Though popular in the United Provinces, Bombay and Madras, social support for the League were still fairly weak in **three of the provinces from which Pakistan was to be carved out just ten years later – Bengal, the NWFP and the Punjab.**

6. b The "Muslim mass contact" was launched by Congress but it did not achieve any substantial gains in the "Muslim mass contact" programme it launched.

7. c **Sikandar Hayat Khan, Punjab Premier and leader of the Unionist Party, w**ho had drafted the resolution, declared in a Punjab assembly speech on 1 March 1941 that he was opposed to a Pakistan that would mean "Muslim Raj here and Hindu Raj elsewhere.

8. a The origins of the Pakistan demand have also been traced back to the Urdu poet Mohammad Iqbal, the writer of "Sare Jahan Se Achha Hindustan Hamara".

9. c When negotiations were begun again in 1945, the British agreed to create an entirely Indian central Executive Council, except for the Viceroy and the Commander-in-Chief of the armed forces, as a preliminary step towards full independence.

10. c Discussions about the transfer of power broke down due to Jinnah's unrelenting demand that the League had an absolute right to choose all the Muslim members of the Executive Council and that there should be a kind of communal veto in the Council

Level – 2

11. c Arya Samaj: A North Indian Hindu reform organisation of the late nineteenth and early twentieth centuries, particularly active in the Punjab, **which sought to revive Vedic learning and combine it with modern education in the sciences.**

12 d Scholars suggest that separate electorates for Muslims, **created by the colonial government in 1909 and expanded in 1919,** crucially shaped the nature of communal politics.

Separate electorates created a temptation for politicians working within this system to use sectarian slogans and gather a following by distributing favours to their own religious groups.

Communal identities were consolidated by a host of other developments in the early twentieth century. **Muslims were angered by "music-before-mosque", by the cow protection movement, and by the efforts of the Arya Samaj to bring back to the Hindu fold (*shuddhi*) those who had recently converted to Islam.**

13. a Only the first statement is correct.

Only about 10 to 12 per cent of the population enjoyed the right to vote. The Congress did well in the elections, winning an **absolute majority in five out of eleven provinces** and forming **governments in seven of them.** It did badly in the constituencies reserved for **Muslims, but the Muslim League also fared poorly,**

14. c The Congress ministries also contributed to the widening rift. In the United Provinces, the party had rejected the **Muslim League proposal for a**

coalition government partly because the League tended to support landlordism, which the Congress wished to abolish, although the party had not yet taken any concrete steps in that direction.

15. d Maulana Azad, an important Congress leader, pointed out in **1937** that members of the Congress were not allowed to join the League

Only in December **1938** did the Congress Working Committee declare that Congress members could not be members of the Mahasabha.

16. c The Pakistan demand was formalised gradually. On 23 March 1940, the League moved a resolution **demanding a measure of autonomy for the Muslim- majority areas of the subcontinent. This ambiguous resolution never mentioned partition or Pakistan**

17. c

18. c Provincial elections were again held in 1946. The Congress swept the general constituencies, capturing 91.3 per cent of the non-Muslim vote. The League's success in the seats reserved for Muslims was equally spectacular: it won all 30 reserved constituencies in the Centre with 86.6 per cent of the Muslim vote and 442 out of 509 seats in the provinces. However, the franchise was extremely limited. About 10 to 12 per cent of the population enjoyed the right to vote in the provincial elections and a mere one per cent in the elections for the Central Assembly. Therefore it was not even possible for 80% of Muslim population to vote in the first place. Hence, the statement d is incorrect.

19. d In March 1946 the British Cabinet sent a three-member mission to Delhi to examine the League's demand

Recommendation by the Cabinet Mission: **India was to remain united.** It was to have a weak central government controlling only foreign affairs, defence and communications with the existing provincial assemblies being grouped into three sections while electing the constituent assembly: Section A for the Hindu- majority provinces, and Sections B and C for the Muslim-majority provinces of the north-west and the north-east (including Assam) respectively.

They would have the power to set up intermediate-level executives and legislatures of their own

Initially, all the major parties accepted this plan. But the agreement was short-lived because it was based on mutually opposed interpretations of the plan.

Ultimately, therefore, neither the League nor the Congress agreed to the Cabinet Mission's proposal.

20. d Both the statements are incorrect.

In the 1936 elections, the League **failed to win a single seat in the North-West Frontier** Province (NWFP) and could capture **only two out of 84 reserved constituencies in the Punjab and three out of 33 in Sind.**

CHAPTER 15

THEME FIFTEEN

Framing the Constitution

The Beginning of a New Era

1. A Tumultuous Time

- The years immediately preceding the making of the Constitution had been exceptionally tumultuous
- The Great Calcutta Killings of August 1946 began a year of almost continuous rioting across northern and eastern India
- The violence culminated in the massacres that accompanied the transfer of populations when the Partition of India was announced.
- Another, and scarcely less serious, problem faced by the new nation was that of the princely states.
- This was the background in which the Constituent Assembly met.

The making of the Constituent Assembly

- The members of the Constituent Assembly were not elected on the basis of universal franchise.
- In the winter of 1945-46 provincial elections were held in India.
- The Provincial Legislatures then chose the representatives to the Constituent Assembly.
- The Constituent Assembly that came into being was dominated by one party: the Congress.
- The Congress swept the general seats in the provincial elections, and the Muslim League captured most of the reserved Muslim seats.
- But the League chose to boycott the Constituent Assembly, pressing its demand for Pakistan with a separate constitution.
- 82 per cent of the members of the Constituent Assembly were also members of the Congress.
- The Congress however was not a party with one voice. Its members differed in their opinion on critical issues.
- The discussions within the Constituent Assembly were also influenced by the opinions expressed by the public.
- As the deliberations continued, the arguments were reported in newspapers, and the proposals were publicly debated.

- Important issues of cultural rights and social justice raised in these public discussions were debated on the floor of the Assembly.

The dominant voices

- The Constituent Assembly had 300 members.
- Of these, six members played particularly important roles.
- Three were representatives of the Congress, namely, Jawaharlal Nehru, Vallabh Bhai Patel and Rajendra Prasad.
- Nehru -moved the crucial "Objectives Resolution", as well as the resolution proposing that the National Flag of India be a "horizontal tricolour of saffron, white and dark green in equal proportion", with a wheel in navy blue at the centre.
- Patel - worked mostly behind the scenes, playing a key role in the drafting of several reports
- Rajendra Prasad - As President of the Assembly, he had to steer the discussion
- Besides this Congress trio, a very important member of the Assembly was the lawyer and economist B.R. Ambedkar.
- He served as Chairman of the Drafting Committee of the Constitution.
- Serving with him were two other lawyers, K.M. Munshi and Alladi Krishnaswamy Aiyar
- Ambedkar himself had the responsibility of guiding the Draft Constitution through the Assembly.
- This took three years in all, with the printed record of the discussions taking up eleven bulky volumes.

2. The Vision of the Constitution

- On 13 December 1946, Jawaharlal Nehru introduced the "Objectives Resolution" in the Constituent Assembly.
- It was a momentous resolution that outlined the defining ideals of the Constitution of Independent India, and provided the framework within which the work of constitution-making was to proceed.

- It proclaimed India to be an "Independent Sovereign Republic", guaranteed its citizens justice, equality and freedom, and assured that "adequate safeguards shall be provided for minorities, backward and tribal areas, and Depressed and Other Backward Classes

- The Constituent Assembly was expected to express the aspirations of those who had participated in the movement for independence.

- The British had been forced to introduce a series of constitutional reforms.

- A number of Acts were passed (1909, 1919 and 1935), gradually enlarging the space for Indian participation in provincial governments.

- When elections were held in 1937, under the 1935 Act, the Congress came to power in eight out of the 11 provinces.

3. Defining Rights

The Problem with Separate Electorates

- On 27 August 1947, B. Pocker Bahadur from Madras made a powerful plea for continuing separate electorates.

- This demand for separate electorates provoked anger and dismay amongst most nationalists.

- Not all Muslims supported the demand for separate electorates.

- Some felt that separate electorates were self-destructive since they isolated the minorities from the majority.

- By 1949, most Muslim members of the Constituent Assembly were agreed that separate electorates were against the interests of the minorities.

- Instead Muslims needed to take an active part in the democratic process to ensure that they had a decisive voice in the political system.

Rights of the Depressed Castes

- Numerically the Depressed Castes were not a minority: they formed between 20 and 25 per cent of the total population.

- Their suffering was due to their systematic marginalisation, not their numerical insignificance. They had no access to education, no share in the administration.

- The Constituent Assembly finally recommended that untouchability be abolished, Hindu temples be thrown open to all castes, and seats in legislatures and jobs in government offices be reserved for the lowest castes.

4. The Powers of the State

- One of the topics most vigorously debated in the Constituent Assembly was the respective rights of the Central Government and the states

- The Draft Constitution provided for three lists of subjects: Union, State, and Concurrent.

- The subjects in the first list were to be the preserve of the Central Government, while those in the second list were vested with the states.

- As for the third list, here Centre and state shared responsibility.

- The Union also had control of minerals and key industries.

- Besides, Article 356 gave the Centre the powers to take over a state administration on the recommendation of the Governor.

- In the case of some taxes (for instance, customs duties and Company taxes) the Centre retained all the proceeds; in other cases (such as income tax and excise duties) it shared them with the states; in still other cases (for instance, estate duties) it assigned them wholly to the states.

- The states, meanwhile, could levy and collect certain taxes on their own: these included land and property taxes, sales tax, and the hugely profitable tax on bottled liquor.

What we want today is a strong Government

- Ambedkar had declared that he wanted "a strong and united Centre , much stronger than the Centre we had created under the Government of India Act of 1935".

5. The Language of the Nation

- By the 1930s, the Congress had accepted that Hindustani ought to be the national language. Hindustani – a blend of Hindi and Urdu – was a popular language of a large section of the people of India

- From the end of the nineteenth century, however, Hindustani as a language had been gradually changing.

- As communal conflicts deepened, Hindi and Urdu also started growing apart.

A plea for Hindi

- The Language Committee of the Constituent Assembly decided, but not yet formally declared, that Hindi in the Devanagari script would be the official language, but the transition to Hindi would be gradual.

- For the first fifteen years, English would continue to be used for all official purposes.

- Each province was to be allowed to choose one of the regional languages for official work within the province.

- By referring to Hindi as the official rather that the national language, the Language Committee of the Constituent Assembly hoped to placate ruffled emotions and arrive at a solution that would be acceptable to all.

Exercise

Level – 1

1. Long years ago we made a tryst with destiny, and now the time comes when we shall redeem our pledge

   This famous speech was given by who among the following leaders?

   (a) Jawaharlal Nehru

   (b) Motilal Nehru

   (c) Subhas Chandra Bose

   (d) Rajendra Prasad

2. The members of the Constituent Assembly were elected on the basis of

   (a) Universal franchise

   (b) Through provincial elections

   (c) First Past the post system

   (d) None of the above

3. Consider the following statements

   1. The Constituent Assembly was dominated by Congress Party

   2. Muslim League captured most of the reserved Muslim seats.

   Choose the correct answer using the code below

   (a) 1 Only   (b) 2 Only

   (c) Both 1 and 2   (d) Neither 1 nor 2

4. Find the correct statement about the Constituent assembly

   (a) 60 per cent of the members of the Constituent Assembly were also members of the Congress.

   (b) Muslim League and The Socialists chose to boycott the Constituent Assembly

   (c) Constituent Assembly was a creation of the British

   (d) None of the above

5. The Constituent Assembly had __________ members.

   (a) 198   (b) 178

   (c) 300   (d) 288

6. Who among the following leaders were the representatives of the Congress in the Constituent assembly

   1. Jawaharlal Nehru

   2. Vallabh Bhai Patel

   3. Rajendra Prasad

   4. B.R. Ambedkar.

Choose the correct answer from the codes given below:

   (a) 1, 2 and 3 only   (b) 2, 3 and 4 only

   (c) 1, 3 and 4 only   (d) 1, 2, 3 and 4

7. Objectives Resolution was moved by who among the following leaders

   (a) Jawaharlal Nehru   (b) Rajendra Prasad

   (c) Vallabh Bhai Patel   (d) Sacchidanand Sinha

8. The resolution proposing that the National Flag of India be a "horizontal tricolour of saffron, white and dark green in equal proportion", was moved by

   ____

   (a) Mahatma Gandhi

   (b) K.M. Munshi

   (c) Alladi Krishnaswamy Aiyar

   (d) None of the above

9. Who among the following leaders had the responsibility of guiding the Draft Constitution through the Assembly?

   (a) S. N. Mukherjee   (b) B.R Ambedkar

   (c) Jawahar Lal Nehru   (d) Rajendra Prasad

10. Which of the following term was not used by Jawaharlal Nehru in the Objectives Resolution

   (a) Democratic   (b) Republic

   (c) Sovereign   (d) Both a and b

Level – 2

11. The executive was made entirely responsible to the provincial legislature through which of the following acts?

   (a) Government of India Act of 1935.

   (b) Indian Councils Act 1909

   (c) Indian Councils Act 1909

   (d) The 1947 Indian Independence Act

12. The legislatures elected under the 1935 Act operated within the framework of colonial rule, and were responsible to the ______________ appointed by the British

   (a) Governor   (b) Governor General

   (c) Viceroy   (d) Interim governor

13. Find the correct statement with reference to the Elections of 1937

   (a) The elections were held in 1937, under the 1935 Act

(b) In this election the Congress came to power in eight out of the 11 provinces.

(c) There was no universal adult franchise.

(d) All of the above

14. Direct action day was announced by which of the following organisations/leaders?

(a) Muslim League   (b) Mahatma Gandhi

(c) Hindu Mahasabha   (d) Rajputanas

15. Hindustani language is a blend of _____________ and _____________

(a) Hindi and Urdu   (b) Hindi. and Sanskrit

(c) Sanskrit and Urdu   (d) Hindi and Persian

16. Find the correct statement with respect to tax regime

(a) Centre shares income tax and customs duties with the states

(b) The states, could levy and collect land and property taxes

(c) In the case of taxes like excise duties the Centre retained all the proceeds

(d) None of the above

17. Which of the following articles gave the power to the Centre to take over a state administration on the recommendation of the Governor.

(a) Article 356

(b) Article 352

(c) Article 360

(d) Article 358

18. During the period of British rule, he had been a political opponent of the Congress; but, on the advice of Mahatma Gandhi, he was asked to join the Union Cabinet as law minister after independence.

The above statement best describes which of the following leaders:

(a) B. N. Rau

(b) B.R Ambedkar

(c) Subhash Chandra Bose

(d) S. N. Mukherjee

Answers

Level-1

1. (a)   **2.** (b)   **3.** (c)   **4.** (d)   **5.** (c)   **6.** (a)   **7.** (a)   **8.** (d)   **9.** (b)   **10.** (a)

Level-2

11. (a)   **12.** (a)   **13.** (d)   **14.** (a)   **15.** (a)   **16.** (b)   **17.** (a)   **18.** (b)

Explanations

Level – 1

1. a • *Jawaharlal Nehru* gave his famous speech that began with the following lines:

"Long years ago we made a tryst with destiny, and now the time comes when we shall redeem our pledge, not wholly or in full measure, but very substantially. At the stroke of the midnight hour, when the world sleeps, India will awake to life and freedom."

2. b • The members of the Constituent Assembly were not elected on the basis of universal franchise. In the winter of 1945-46 provincial elections were held in India. The Provincial Legislatures then chose the representatives to the Constituent Assembly.

3. c • Congress swept the general seats in the provincial elections, and the Muslim League captured most of the reserved Muslim seats.

4. d • Muslim League chose to boycott the Constituent Assembly, pressing its demand for Pakistan with a separate constitution.

• The Socialists too were initially unwilling to join, for they believed the Constituent Assembly was a creation of the British, and therefore incapable of being truly autonomous.

• 82 per cent of the members of the Constituent Assembly were also members of the Congress.

5. c • The Constituent Assembly had 300 members.

6. a • The Constituent Assembly had 300 members. Of these, six members played particularly important roles. Three were representatives of the Congress, namely, Jawaharlal Nehru, Vallabh Bhai Patel and Rajendra Prasad.

7. a • It was Nehru who moved the crucial Objectives Resolution

8. d • It was Nehru who moved the resolution proposing that the National Flag of India be a "horizontal tricolour of saffron, white and dark green in equal proportion", with a wheel in navy blue at the centre.

9. b • Ambedkar had the responsibility of guiding the Draft Constitution through the Assembly.

10. a • Jawaharlal Nehru didn't use the term "democratic" in the Objectives Resolution

Level – 2

11. a • The executive was made partly responsible to the provincial legislature in 1919, and almost entirely so under the Government of India Act of 1935.

12. a The legislatures elected under the 1935 Act operated within the framework of colonial rule, and were responsible to the Governor appointed by the British.

13. d

14. a • Muslim League announces Direct Action Day

15. a • Hindustani – a blend of Hindi and Urdu – was a popular language of a large section of the people of India, and it was a composite language enriched by the interaction of diverse cultures.

16. b • In the case of some taxes (for instance, customs duties and Company taxes) the Centre retained all the proceeds; in other cases (such as income tax and excise duties) it shared them with the states; in still other cases (for instance, estate duties) it assigned them wholly to the states. The states, meanwhile, could levy and collect certain taxes on their own: these included land and property taxes, sales tax, and the hugely profitable tax on bottled liquor.

17. a • Article 356 gave the Centre the powers to take over a state administration on the recommendation of the Governor.

18. b

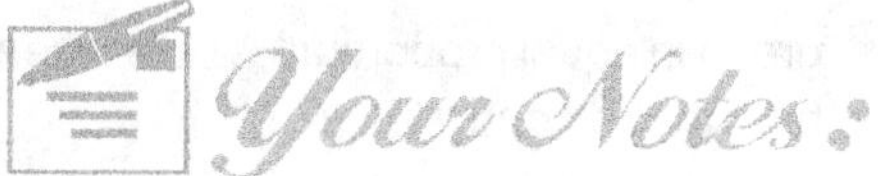 *Your Notes :* ....